Jean-Pierre Benamou

10 MILLION TONS FOR VICTORY

The Arsenal of Democracy

During

The Battle of France in 1944

Translated by Ms Lesley COUTTS M.A. (Hons), D.E.S.S. - With the collaboration of Ms Véronique MAUGER.

Général de Gaulle,
22 juin 1940 :
« ... We still have
the gigantic possibilities of
American Industry.
The same conditions of war
which led us to be beaten
by 5,000 planes
and 6,000 tanks may tomorrow
bring victory by 20,000 tanks
and 20,000 planes. »

Rearmed through the American war effort, the 2nd French armoured division
is ready for the battle for France in 1944.

Contents

Loading of the upper bridge
of a US naval LST.

1944 marked the restoration of the freedom, which Europe was unable to preserve in 1940 when faced with the Nazi hegemony of Adolf Hitler's IIIrd Reich. The honours of this new found freedom must be paid to the soldiers of the Liberation and to the combat units who launched the assault on the beaches and the Norman bocage and who, today, are part of the legend of the Normandy Landings.

Yet behind each soldier, sailor or airman launched at the spearhead of the Battle of Normandy, then throughout the Battle for France, 10 other soldiers standing in the shadows gave them the opportunity to reach their objectives, taking as few risks as possible, as quickly and comfortably as possible.

The soldiers of American logistics alone represented 80 % of the US support forces from spring to winter 1944 in France. They were the product of American industry, thrown into the fight against Nazi war production, first in Normandy, then throughout France : soldiers in port battalions, dockers in uniform, chauffeurs, machine drivers, navvies-quartermasters, storemen, specialized workers, railwaymen, surgeons, medical staff, chemists, telegraphists and other cobblers and armourers all present to serve the same ideal of democracy "made in the USA".

These were the troops of the Canadian, British and American war effort, named "the rear", who in their task of providing logistical support, enabled the Allied victory in Europe in 1945. For we must not forget the civilian craftsmen, 65 million men and women, united in a vast industrial enterprise, to forge the tools of victory.

BEFORE CONTINENTAL EUROPE,
the UNITED KINGDOM

The retreat from Dunkerque of the British Expeditionary Corps in June 1940, among which figured General Montgomery's troops who'd faced those of General Guderian and General Rommel, who surged through Paris, enabled the "invincible Albion" to remain just that. Thanks to the leasing law signed between the USA and Great Britain, 270,000 British, French, Belgian, Polish, Norwegian, Czech and Dutch troops were rearmed to face the possible German invasion of the British Isles. Yet this Battle, which became known as the Battle of Britain, came from above. In August and September 1940, the white trails left by the planes were the only signs of the dog fights which were to lead to the defeat of Field Marshall Goering's Luftwaffe and to the German High Command decision to abandon plans to land on the beaches of the South coasts of England. The new Prime Minister, Winston Churchill, became the personification of the will to resist the Nazis and to preserve the integrity of the United Kingdom, the only Western base available to coalition forces if, one day, they were to return to Europe. Prime Minister and First Resistance Fighter, Winston Churchill honoured his international fighter pilots by admitting in the House of Commons that "never in the field of human conflict has so much been owed by so many to so few", whilst recalling that "if the British Empire and Commonwealth were to survive one thousand years, people would say those were our finest hours".

① UNITED KINGDOM, MARCH 1944

From this point on, the British Isles were so full of material and equipment of all descriptions, manufactured in the United Kingdom, the USA and Canada, that "it was said to be the effect of the anti-aircraft captive balloons, floating in the air, which have prevented the isles from sinking !" Three million soldiers were divided among numerous training centres, which were constantly strengthened by the continuous arrival of GIs, recruits in the new, young USA army under the presidency of Franklin Delano Roosevelt. The frequency of the arrivals of transatlantic cruise ships, forming long convoys, which attracted the attention of the Nazi submarines, brought some 216,700 GIs into the country per month. The two "queens" alone, the Queen Elizabeth and the Queen Mary each transported some 15,000 men per trip, totalling some 425,000 for D-Day !

Winston Churchill welcomed them thus : "Here you are on this little island surrounded by Northern mists. I cannot give you any guarantees on the weather, but can guarantee that you will be welcomed by warm hearts". Another convoy of 24 merchant naval ships and 18 cargo ships at the end of March brought 1,500 vehicles, tanks and self-propelled guns, 2,000 vehicles in crates, 200 planes and gliders with 50,000 tons of freight. One week later, the 1st American Army had absorbed this equipment transporting it from quayside to the depots in 19,000 wagons, which made up 100 trains.

The gigantic arsenal of democracy brought in from the USA.

In England, a park of vehicles
in crates close to an American transport glider runway.

*Guess who was
camped here in England !* ▶

"They won't let on who the camp is for."

ACANTHUS

② UNITED KINGDOM, MAY 1944

1,527,000 GIs had arrived in England, while the frequency of supplies from the USA alone reached 2 million tons per month until and throughout the summer of 1944. During this same period, the British government pursued its help to Soviet Russia on the base of 100,000 tons per month, while a good number of sovereign nations, who were free from all oppression, also took part in the world effort.

By the end of May, on Winston Churchill's "little island", the American "Bolero" plan to accommodate and support 2,021,387 Allied soldiers was operational. British citizens accommodated 500,000 soldiers from Scotland to Kent. Over and above this, in their arsenals, the sailors of the Royal Navy added some 600,000 men and women to the numbers. On their numerous bases, the airmen of the RAF, the Commonwealth, and the crews of 25 other Allied nations amounted to another million !

The Bolero plan above included the accommodation of 442,170 American airmen, 372,668 soldiers chosen for D-Day (in special camps) and 1,206,349 American soldiers, both men and women.

BEFORE CONTINENTAL EUROPE
the UNITED KINGDOM

Near Lison, an American general hospital. In the centre, the surgical blocks in Nissen huts.

Accommodation was provided in semi-circular corrugated iron Nissen huts, built on stone foundations and with wooden interiors.

Each Nissen camp was to host 1,000 men. Built over 40 hectares, 123 buildings were used for sleeping barracks, but also for administrative purposes with numerous offices, the mess, showers, canteens, sports halls and medical facilities.

The less fortunate had to camp. The "tent camps" for 1,000 men were each pitched on 34 hectares of land with 200 campaign tents, allowing standing height. The inevitable "Bolero" mobile hospitals and 31 others in civilian or military buildings, were spread throughout accommodation zones, with a total capacity of 84,210 beds !

A standard American general hospital included 160 buildings (Nissen huts) and large marquees over some 50 hectares with a capacity of 1,082 beds and 2,800 medical staff. The British model was more modest, with 660 beds and 1,500 medical staff.

To feed these forces, the British took care of the American camps, with the help of 38 American groups of bakeries, and used 250,000 tons of flour per day, imported from the USA and Canada, and this was only sufficient for 60 % of the needs of the American army above !

The airmen, based on 126 American airfields, were supplied exclusively with British produce : this was also true for fuel and flight equipment, from goggles to the Horsa gliders with 4,500 km of Sommerfeldt tracks for take-off runways, 50 maintenance workshops and … 1,200 pubs with beer bearing the army stamp. Special treatment was given to the GIs by the British population, who took care of "their" Americans, much to the regret of the British soldiers who found them "too present (over there), too well-paid (over-paid) and too often with their women (over-sexed)".

At the end of May 1944, the American army lived off 63 % of British produce, which provided it with 83 campaign bakeries, clothes, uniforms, various equipment, 15 million jerrycans, but also Bailey bridges, railways and various building constructions. In order to reach "H" hour on "D" day, 6th June 1944, British workers had worked for 400 million hours, 20 % of those in the secret building of the elements of the Mulberry harbours.

BEFORE CONTINENTAL EUROPE

Finally, 130,000 American vehicles in parts were assembled by civilians in June 1944. From January to June, they were also to provide the Americans with the service of 9,225 special trains composed of some 950,000 wagons in accordance with the leasing agreement the terms of which were "for the unique benefit of quick and final victory".

In accordance with the "mutual aid" agreement, the British population provided the American troops in preparation for Overlord with some 3,851,000 tons of food tanks to 100,000 British workers exclusively involved in the American war effort, although financed by the British Ministry of War. President Roosevelt himself was to evaluate the industrial contribution of the "little island" in favour of the American army to the equivalent of 1,000 trans-Atlantic merchant naval ships.

American General Lee (on left) in charge of all American supplies for Europe. He is here congratulated by General Eisenhower.

③ 3RD JUNE 1944

Under the supreme command of General Dwight David Eisenhower, the American General Lee transferred most of the logistics under his command to the continent in support of the 1.2 million GIs who landed in Normandy up until August 15th 1944. During August, over 5 million tons of military equipment and supplies were spread throughout Anglo-American parks and depot zones just inside the Atlantic Wall, which collapsed from Cherbourg to Cabourg following the colossal naval, air and land battles of D-Day.

Light armoured vehicles, American Staghounds on the left, British Humber on the right.

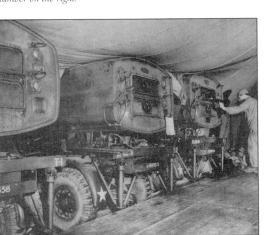

The American Army's mobile campaign bakeries which produced around 2 million tons of bread during the liberation of Europe.

The LOGISTICS of the ARMIES of the LIBERATION

Logistics is the sum of operations, the aim of which are to enable armies to be fed, manoeuvre, fight, ensure evacuation and medical treatment for their personnel. The Anglo-Saxon Ordnance or Supply Corps, fuel or POL "Petrol, Oil and Lubricants", materials and munitions, health service or Medical Department.
Classification :
- Class I = food supplies.
- Class II = individuals' equipment.
- Class III = fuel provision (petrol for the army, the air force and diesel, plus lubricants).
- Class IV = engineering equipment and transmissions.
- Class V munitions.

Winston Churchill addressing the Commons :
"Supplies are the lifeblood of our armies !"

The role of the Ordnance Corps was to ensure the provision of the necessary supplies and munitions, in sufficient quantities, in the right place at the right time, when the army needed them. The variety included in the word "supplies" is surprising, from the toothbrush to the tank carrier and from the cartridge to an anti-aircraft radar !
In the course of Overlord and plan Neptune, its naval component, it was up to the Allied Merchant Navy, under the protection of His Majesty's Royal Navy, to transport the entire supplies for General Montgomery's 21st group of armies from the South Coast of England to the beaches and ports of the Normandy Coast. A good twenty or so nations armed and chartered those merchant ships, which were a mix of coasters, tankers, all types of cargo ships along with the American "Liberty Ships", which were built in one year at the speed of 2 units per day by 5,000 workers.

❶ THE OPERATIONAL SUPPLY PLAN FOR OVERLORD

The Trans-Atlantic convoys and then the cross-Channel shuttles from Falmouth along the English coast to Portsmouth, all headed for the selected Normandy beaches :
- Utah Beach, opened by the 7th US Army Corps ;
- Omaha Beach, opened by the 5th US Army Corps ;
- Gold Beach, opened by the 30th British Army Corps ;
- Juno Beach, opened by the Canadian Army Sword Beach, opened by the 1st British Army Corps.
The small harbours of St Vaast-la-Hougue, Barfleur, Isigny, Grandcamp, Port en Bessin, Courseulles sur Mer were all to play a major role before the capture of Cherbourg (27th June) and the hypothetical reparation of its port installations (at the beginning of August). The major ports of St.Malo and Brest, superior in capacity, had been included in the American logistics plan, as was the Quiberon Bay, but they were never to be used, as, by the time they had fallen after long sieges, they were too far removed from the front.

As Lord Louis Mountbatten, Admiral of the Fleet, had planned and imagined as early as 1942, given the uncertainty of capturing a port in good working order, the Allies would have to build one and tug it across the Channel before assembling it on the consolidated bridgehead. The gigantic building site began in 1943, of course in strangely kept secrecy ; according to the father of the Overlord programme, General Morgan, whilst half of England and a large part of Ireland seemed to be working on the bizarrely code-named "Mulberries".

▲ *American ordnance park and different types of Sherman tanks.*

◄ January/February 1944, the Thames estuary : construction of blocks ships for the Norman artificial ports.

The problem faced by the Joint Chiefs of Staff of the Supreme Allied Command (COSSAC) was simple : the rate of the supplies to the troops in Normandy had to be superior to that of the opposition, despite the lack of major ports, and this had to be the case, in the long term, until the Allies reached the Seine (2nd British army under General "Bimbo" Dempsey) before D-Day + 90. This was why it became necessary to drag 2 major prefabricated floating harbours the product of British ingeniosity (Commodore John H. Hallett), under the auspices of Winston Churchill, to Normandy with the troops. Cherbourg, at best, by the end of June, could have handled 3,750 tons daily, but the town was still occupied by the Von Schielen Command. On top of this, statistics from one meteorological department of the British Admiralty showed that in

June, the beaches of Lower-Normandy were, on average unusable for 6 days ! The devastating storm, which began on the 19th June was to end on the 23rd, leaving in its wake the destruction of which, today, we are all aware : the loss of the American Mulberry on Omaha and a considerable delay in maritime transport.

Operation Neptune was daring enough, given the great foresight of the Chiefs of Staff, to plan a spectacular counter-measure against the bad weather : "Gooseberries", the rows of breakwater ships sunk just off the beaches and block ships, cubes of massive concrete dragged by American tugs to their chosen site after having been brought across the 130 km of the English Channel. Though less spectacular than the Mulberrry harbours, the "Gooseberries" made up of some 40 to 70 ships, were scuppered over 1,500 m, one mile off shore from the beaches and provided the best shelter from the waves for the five Landing Beaches, each of approximately 7 km in length.

The LOGISTICS of the ARMIES of the LIBERATION

② THE DEVELOPMENT OF THE LOGISTICAL OPERATION

7 days' bad weather had been expected. They were faced with 3 weeks' rain, wind and low clouds, which caused difficulties for the approaching ships, destroyed Mulberry "A" (American) and halted the air support, so essential to the success of land operations on the narrow Norman beachhead.

A - BEFORE THE STORM OF THE CENTURY (19TH – 22ND JUNE)

There was a delay on Omaha, thus preventing US engineers from completely freeing, securing and dominating a beach in this area until June 10th. The coasters were the backbone of the supply forces ; each was able to transport from 200 to 2,000 tons of supplies and they arrived as early as the 2nd tide on the 6th June. They constituted the vanguard of the 126 pre-loaded units of 90,000 tons for the 1st US Army under General Bradley.

Around the same time, 18 LCTs cruised at sea awaiting the freeing of a beach around 1.00 pm on D-Day to land 140 tons of divisionary reserves. The first provisional depot at Omaha was set up at the foot of the plateau in Saint Laurent, then in Colleville-sur-Mer, on D-Day + 2. The planned frequency of supplies for Omaha was of 3,000 tons and of 2,500 tons for Utah during the days following the Landings. Utah alone was to meet with these expectations until the opening of Mulberry "A" on June 17th, reaching 5,000 tons and 1,500 vehicles per day thanks to the 4 km² of landing stages for 5 cargo ships, 7 coasters and 7 liberty ships.

The effect of the "storm of the century" on the artificial harbour in Arromanches, which survived the worst of the storm and was later to be strengthened with parts from the Omaha harbour which had been abandoned. ▾

JUNE

A FRENZIED BATTLE AS MUCH AGAINST BAD WEATHER AS AGAINST THE ENEMY

B - THE STORM

On June 19th, the 3 km of floating roads were the first to give way, quickly becoming projectiles. Admiral Tennant's 2 Mulberries, technological miracles in themselves, were insufficient when faced with mother Nature's rage. Mulberry A was devastated within 72 hours, but Mulberry B (British) at Arromanches was better protected in a cove, favoured by local fishermen, where it withstood the elements and survived : 30 % of the replacement parts required were elements of Mulberry A, to be abandoned by the Allies thus enabling the town of Arromanches to enter into the History of army logistics. The sailors of the Merchant Navy served on 2,000 commercial vessels, excluding the 5,000 units launched during Operation Neptune (thus equivalent to moving 4,000,000 barrels).

The 70,000 members of the Merchant Navy forgot their sailors' privileges to become soldiers, very much aware that they were taking on the largest humanitarian and military enterprise of the 20th Century.

◀ *Omaha Beach : LSTs used for transporting supplies lie wrecked on the beach.*

The beach in Arromanches after the storm.
▼

▲ *The storm on July 19th, 1944 in Arromanches.*

The LOGISTICS of the ARMIES of the LIBERATION

C - AFTER THE STORM

Morosity had set in amongst the Allied forces. After the initial victory of the combined Land-Air-Sea forces, the Americans got caught up in the bocage area of the Manche County where every hedgerow was fiercely held by the German paratroopers waiting in ambush around St. Lô. The main objective on the Cotentin peninsula was the port of Cherbourg, which had been transformed into a fortress by the "Kriegsmarine" with the support of the Wehrmacht. The Anglo-Canadians around Caen, former D-Day objective, were pushed back by the "Waffen-SS" and by the "Panzer-Lehr Division", the "Crème" of Rommel's forces.

As it never rains but it pours, low clouds set in and the bombers were unable to risk attacking. The fighters were blocked on their advanced airfields, transformed into quagmires by gusts of rain and western winds from Ste Mère l'Eglise to Bayeux. Moreover, the 1st American and 2nd British armies, growing in numbers, had to be rationed from this point onwards.

Bradley and Demspey, filled with dismay, complained to their Chief of Operations, Montgomery. Unruffled, he tried to reassure them that "all was well". The truth, however, was that 325,000 men had landed in France (on the 22nd June) as opposed to the 385,000 initially planned, with 45,000 tons in reserve as opposed to 70,000 planned. The storm alone reduced the speed of the landings by 60 % and even if Class I supplies (food) were in sufficient quantity in the depots, some muni-

▲ *View of Omaha from Colleville/Mer.*

tions for the artillery (105 mm) and the infantry (mortar) were dangerously lacking. In the hedgerows, orders were given to repost only when there was the certainty of enemy fire and, when possible, to recuperate arms and munitions abandoned by the enemy.

On Omaha, 1,500 soldiers of the Engineers Corps were employed for a whole week clearing the debris of the pontoons, landing craft, ships and various elements projected along the coast, blocking access to the beaches, so vital to bring supplies ashore.

100 LCVPs and LCMs (assault landing craft) were lost along with

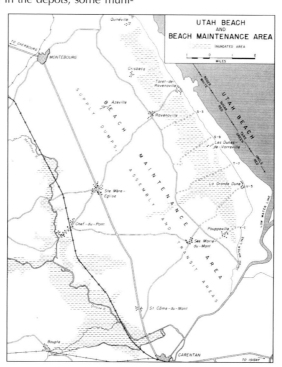
◄ *Utah Beach.*

around 20 tank transporting crafts (LCTs) and all of the rhino ferries or motorized pontoons.

Opposite Exit E3, no less than 35 LCMs, 11 LCTs, 9 rhinoferries, 3 LCIs and other dismantled DUKWs lay entangled, washed up on the sand.

Utah Beach was less open to the West wind and from June 21st onward, the shuttle of coasters was able to operate once again as normal. On June 23rd, the US Navy, doubling its energy when faced with adversity and helped by the Engineer Corps, succeeded in beating the record of tonnage landed since D-Day with 6,500 tons on Utah and 10,000 tons on

NORMANDY 1944

Statistics for the last week in June :
- Omaha = 13,500 tons / day, ie. 115 % of the plan ;
- Utah = 7,000 tons / day, ie 124 % of estimated supplies ;
- Arromanches : 3,600 tons / day, ie 80 % of estimated supplies.

Yet this logistical victory against adversity did not, however, enable the Allies to catch up on the delays caused by the storm and the fall of Cherbourg, later than expected. On June 30th, 290,000 tons were landed on Omaha and Utah as opposed to the 360,000 tons initially planned. The smaller harbours with a more modest debit of 1.000 tons / day were not neglected and the towns of St Vaast-la-Hougue, Grandcamp, Isigny, Carentan and Courseulles continued to dock coasters and light cargos along their quaysides. As far as men were concerned, at this point in the Landings (June 30th) : 452,460 GIs, instead of the 578,971 initially planned, had landed on French soil, i.e. 78 % (under 27,000 were evacuated as injured). On the 4th of July, the millionth soldier landed in Normandy, he was American from the State of Louisiana.

The stagnation of the front in Normandy in June meant that less fuel was used as the distances covered during movements remained modest. Rations (Class I) and munitions (Class V) were priority supplies. In the British sector, where the front was even closer to the coast, the storm had been less rampant and with land operations becoming static, the reduced frequency of supplies had less effect on the troops than in the US sector, which was more widespread.

The port of Caen, initially included in the logistics plan, from the first days of the Landings, was never to be used as planned. It was only made available in August, and by that point, being too late, it became a coal port ! Ouistreham, which is the estuary, was kept under the observation of the Mont Canisy batteries until the 17th of August. Considered too dangerous, this harbour was never used. Every day, a smoke screen was created to hamper enemy fire to the East of the River Orne. The beaches, despite tidal difficulties, were also to play an essential role in this area, with some 4,500 tons / day landing on Gold and 5,200 tons / day on Juno by July 1st, thus superior to the average / beach debit of Mulberry B in Arromanches.

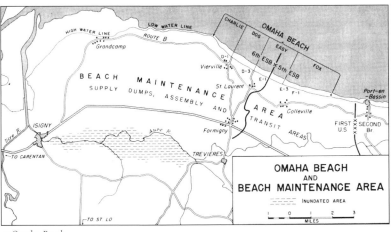

▲ Omaha Beach.

Omaha, which was sadly lacking its artificial harbour. When Cherbourg finally fell, under the joint pressure of Collins 7th Corps, US Naval fire and attacks from the 9th US Air Force, and the overwhelming damage in the city was discovered, those beaches were to remain the best supply beaches, far superior to the surviving artificial harbour at Arromanches (Mulberry B, Port Winston).

The LOGISTICS of the ARMIES of the LIBERATION

③ THE DEPOT ZONES

A - IN THE BRITISH SECTOR

Supply depot n°1 was located in "la Délivrande", with on June 19th, 82 million rations stocked, the equivalent of 2 weeks' reserves (Army road head n° 1).

British rations were kept for the Allied troops other than the Americans (2nd British army and 1st Canadian army). The rations were delivered in wooden crates and boxes for 14 men, with, in each, packed boxes for breakfast, lunch and dinner as well as titbits whilst on the march and for short breaks (tea and biscuits), the tommy cooker was also included. 10 million crates (14 men packs) were produced by the "Ministry of Food" with 7 different varieties to satisfy the international tastes of the troops : pudding, mixed fruit rice pudding, various types of meat dishes in tins, salted salmon, "victory" cigarettes and matches. From June 6th to August 31st 1944, the British depots distributed :

1 billion 200 million cigarettes, 35 million bars of chocolate, 22 million packets of razor blades, 9 million packets of toilet paper (5 pieces for officers, only 3 for the ordinary soldier), 5 million bottles of English Bulldog beer and Irish Guiness, 480,000 bottles of whisky (Black and White, Long John), 600,000 jugs of Navy Rhum, not counting the numerous bottles of champagne and good wine, which were "liberated" !

The first depots on French soil were set up from Ouistreham to Asnelles, immediately inside the German defence zones, just behind the dunes, as early as June 6th. The exiguity of the fray bridgehead made installations such as these dangerous, as the safety rules could not be fully applied, due to a lack of space. On the 7th June, the 3rd DI's depot was bombed. Over and above the loss of 500,000 litres of fuel and 400 tons of munitions, the death of several soldiers was greatly regretted. From the Gooseberries in Courseulles (Juno) and Hermanville (Sword), the amphibious DUKWs shuttled supplies from the cargo ships to the depots.

First line British troops were nourished exclusively on "Compos" in crates for 14 men.

British rations for a medical diet are collected from a British depot by the Royal Navy.

NORMANDY 1944

General Eisenhower :

" From Cherbourg to Caen stretches the largest supply depot ever known in the history of mankind "

As a port was still lacking on June 11ᵗʰ, 10,850 tons of supplies were delivered through these improvised loading zones. 11 DUKW companies, i.e 500 amphibious machines performed, with the Royal Army Service Corps, the unloading of a maximum of 1,000 tons per day, whilst the harbour in Ouistreham remained under enemy observation and was never to be used in the campaign.

On D-Day, 1,900 tons were landed in the British sector.

On D-Day + 55 (31ˢᵗ July), 750,000 tons of supplies and 88,000 tons of fuel were distributed to the depot zones, thus 85 % of the quantities expected.

Supply Corps Reserves

The reserves were located in depots of 8,000 cases, each corresponding to the supplies required by one brigade for 1 month (350 armoured vehicles) ; or engineering equipment in depots of "packages" of 12,000 crates.

• In Vaux-sur-Aure

The Ordnance Depot of the 2ⁿᵈ British Army had reached 20,000 tons at the beginning of July.

• In Thaon

The 1ˢᵗ Canadian Army's depot had reached 380,000 tons of spare parts, engines and various pieces of equipment, during the month of August.

A typical American menu (K-Ration).

MENU No. 3

FOR 5 COMPLETE RATIONS USE CONTENTS OF THIS BOX TOGETHER WITH CANNED GOODS IN BOX MARKED "2ND HALF OF 5 RATIONS"

* * * * * * * * * * * * * * * * * *

————BREAKFAST————

CEREAL	HAM AND EGGS
BISCUITS AND JAM	
COFFEE AND MILK	

————DINNER————

1 K RATION UNIT PER MAN

1 CAN K RATION MEAT PER MAN

————SUPPER————

CORNED BEEF	PEAS
BISCUITS AND BUTTER	
FRUIT BAR	ORANGE DRINK

HALAZONE TABLETS ARE INCLUDED TO PURIFY WATER FOR DRINKING. (SEE DIRECTIONS ON THE BOTTLE.)

LOOK FOR A CAN OPENER IN A SMALL ENVELOPE IN THIS BOX

* * * * * * * * * * * * * * * * * *

◄ *The British Engineering Park in Vaux/Seulles near Bayeux (elements of floating pontoons).*

The LOGISTICS of the ARMIES
of the LIBERATION

• The Camp in Audrieu

This camp was the largest of those of the Royal Army Ordnance Corps in Normandy. It was opened on D-Day + 22, when the 14th Army Ordnance Depot (AOD) was set up along the Paris to Cherbourg railway, in Audrieu, with 25 drained hectares of 450 m², roads made of metal trellising and auxiliary railroads, covering the fields, which the farmers had regretfully been forced to abandon.

The installation of the camp began on June 30th and was completed by July 25th. It provided everything that was required to keep the moral of the troops on a high : clothes of all descriptions, shoes, toothbrushes, all necessities, but also a few "extras" (after shave, condoms, patriotic writing paper, comic strips…).

Strangely, toothbrushes were always the first things to go short. Over 4,000 men worked in this huge depot up until February 1945, with numerous peaks when the demand for replacement engines, new cannons for the tanks or for machine guns suddenly increased.

The hottest alerts were "white hot", "red hot", and "hot". The 14th AOD was strengthened by the 15th and 16th AODs 3 months after D-Day, with French staff and voluntary prisoners-of-war handling the explosives and munitions. Audrieu was to remain the rear base for the British Army up until the port of Antwerp was re-established in January 1945 (Audrieu Main Theatre Base of Supply) ; and this was

the case despite appalling weather conditions which, just as had been the case with the June storm, were the worst of the century (even if Eisenhower claimed that they had no more effect on Allied supplies than a passing wave !). The winter of 1945, with no "hard" protection, was particularly severe.

• The 17th AOD

This AOD was specialized in munitions. It was set up in Vaux-sur-Aure on D-Day + 11 and operated non-stop until D-Day + 100, with in June : 19,139 tons instead of the 39,240 planned, in July : 52,000 tons instead of the 50,000 planned, in August : 57,000 instead of the 55,000 planned.

The 17th British Army depot was built over 100 km and included the 101st Beach Sub Area by Lion-sur-Mer, Cresserons, Hermanville, Le Manoir and the 102nd Beach Sub Area by Courseulles, Bény and Reviers. The 15th Munitions Depot stretched with the 104th Sub Area to Ryes, Le Manoir, Sommervieu to the North of Bayeux. All of these British munition depots were in the open, sheltered by huge camouflage nets, in the middle of the fields. On 4 occasions, a bomb dropped by the Luftwaffe on one of these depots caused several casualties and destroyed 1,000 tons of equipment. But the real danger was from the fall of mortar shells from the anti-aircraft fire of the Allied navies, which bombed the country every night. On July 24th, at "Le Manoir", the mines depot exploded causing a chain of fire over a distance of 2 km, killing 3 people in its wake.

The British Royal Ordnance Corps Camp in Audrieu is the largest of the supply depots in Normandy.

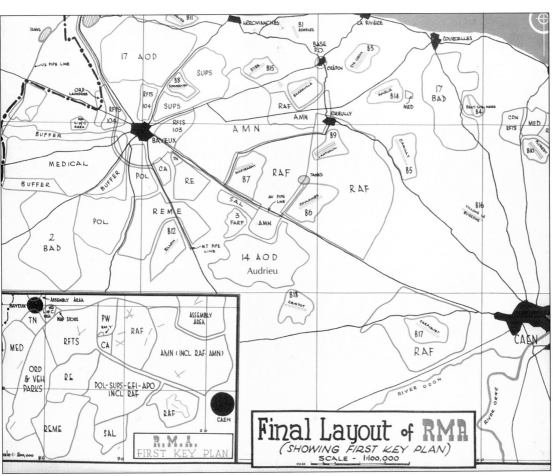

Final Layout of RMA
(SHOWING FIRST KEY PLAN)
SCALE - 1:100,000

R.M.A. FIRST KEY PLAN

- ▸ RAF :   Royal Air Force
- ▸ Bx :   RAF Airfields
- ▸ BAD :   British Army Depots
- ▸ MED :   Medical
- ▸ AMN :   Munitions
- ▸ Tanks :   Reservoirs
- ▸ Buffer :   Demilitarised buffer zone
- ▸ L.O.C. :   Communications line
- ▸ POL :   Petrol Oil Lubricants : lubricants & fuel depots
- ▸ SUPS :   Supplies depot
- ▸ Ord :   Ordnance, artillery & tank depots
- ▸ RFTS :   Reinforcement troops
- ▸ AOD :   Army Ordnance Depot (arms depot)
- ▸ POW :   Prisoners of War
- ▸ Map Stores
- ▸ RE :   Royal Engineers
- ▸ REME :   Royal Electrical and Mechanical Engineers
- ▸ TN :   Training

The LOGISTICS of the ARMIES of the LIBERATION

1) THE DEPOTS

Vehicles arrived in Normandy equipped with their waterproof systems enabling them to land up until the beginning of August. This was additional work for the supplies' teams, who had to ensure that some 130,000 vehicles were waterproof before delivery to the army. Vehicle parks grew like mushrooms, huge areas covered in khaki-coloured mobile equipment, were stocked along side each other down the roads duly reinforced and widened by the Royal Engineers. Over 700 different types of machines from the motorcycle (BSA, Norton, Harley-Davidson or the foldaway British paras' motorcycle) to the trailer or to the Morris tractor or the 25m long armoured Pacific. Light armoured vehicles, bridge builders, flamethrower Churchill tanks and cranes were stocked next to surgical blocks, telephone exchanges, printing factories, campaign garrets, full mobile workshops, bulldozers, scrapers and other motorized wash houses, baths and bakers.

The average exchange stocks reached 45,000 cases per depot, containing engines, vehicle parts and machines, the most recent produced in 1944.

The 17th AOD alone received and distributed 36,000 tons of supplies 24 hours per day from the 24th to 30th June, with the help of 3,000 RASC lorries. On August 5th, the same AOD handled 7,974 tons in 24 hours. From D-Day to D-Day + 72, the 15th and 17th AODs alone stocked some 495,000 tons of munitions, i.e. 6,900 tons per day ! After this period, a rail connection from Courseulles and later Caen, replaced road distribution, as the roads due to heavy traffic and extremely bad weather were in a pitiful condition. The average weight of supply manoeuvred by a soldier of the Allied Supplies Corps every day was of some 7 tons !

THE SUPERB CONTRIBUTION OF THE CANADIAN ARMY TO THE LOGISTICS OF THE LIBERATION

Split over 15 depot zones, the 1st Canadian Army played a brilliant role in the advance from Juno Beach to Dieppe, then to Boulogne, Calais and Ypres, 2 months after Falaise fell to the 2nd Canadian Division.

Well accustomed to driving long distances in all weathers in their 13 home provinces and territories, the Canadian chauffeurs were the most efficient of all the Allied Expeditionary Forces in the Second World War. They had the best results in terms of the distances covered with no major incidents and in terms of the quantity of supplies delivered. The American 3rd Army had, for its part, the lowest efficiency rates in the same conditions. The best case and munitions' packers were also the men of the Royal Canadian Army Service Corps, with an average of 8.7 tons per man per day throughout Operation Overlord. *The Canadian "service guys" were those you could always count on, regardless of circumstances.*

Unloaded directly onto the beaches, these cases of British supplies await their transport by RASC truck to an advanced depot.

2) THE EQUIPMENT
Usual British vehicles in 1944

	Consumption	Fuel tank capacity	Max. speed
Daimler "lynx" Scout car	30 l/100	108 l	80 km/h
Humber Scout car	28 l/100	100 l	95 km/h
Daimler armoured car	17 l/100	85 l	80 km/h
Humbler armoured car	17 l/100	135 l	75 km/h
Ford "Staghound" armoured car (USA)	95 l/100	150 l	90 km/h
Universal Bren Carrier	70 l/100	97 l	50 km/h
General Motors "Sedan" staff car (USA)	16 l/100	63 l	115 km/h
3T Ford Canada truck	15 l/100	100 l	80 km/h
3T Vauxhall truck	28 l/100	120 l	60 km/h
6T Mack Truck	90 l/100	145 l	55 km/h

◄ *British Beach Groups.*

Royal Army Services Corps convoy on the way to the front. ►

▼ *Advanced Canadian depot on Juno Beach.*

The LOGISTICS of the ARMIES of the LIBERATION

B - SUPPLIES – THE AMERICAN MODEL

Stocking, management, distribution and maintenance of munitions were ensured by the materials' department, which was composed of :
- Specialized forces from the army,
- Munitions' companies, each of 6 detachments in charge of operating the depots. The companies' staff managed the workers supplied by the command and the men of transport.

The munitions arrived from the harbours and beaches to the basic supply zones where they were checked, divided up and stocked.

The basic supply depots then provided the supplies to the army depots and intermediary depots.

The army depots in turn provided supplies to the main formations by transfer to delivery and distribution centres. The narrow bridgehead meant that the Allied supply services had to set up their supply zones without respecting the usual safety rules in terms of the spacing out of such zones.

At times, the supply zones were only 400 m apart. 450 tons were blown to ash on the 5th June in Formigny by a rash FW-190 bomb, and then again on the 11th and 12th June. The Navy then built deviation decoys for air attacks such as in St Aubin, Langrune and in the Veys' Bay. Through thin sheets of smoke, barges and vehicles could be seen and although they were all out of use, they were sufficient to attract the attention of the German pilots.

Modern war was most definitely a war of equipment,

The exit from the beach in St Laurent-sur-Mer became a one way road thanks to the efforts of the US Engineers.

where psychological warfare had an essential role to play. The armies' success and the soldiers' survival both were greatly dependent on the successful operation of the supply zone and the Allies' mechanical means.

In Cherbourg, the latest model of brand new Sherman tanks, arrive direct from Connecticut.

NORMANDY 1944

US Air Force Engineers Depot : note the rolls of Sommerfeldt tracks for runways and Square Mesh Tracks.

Unloading of Class I supplies on Omaha Beach.

The LOGISTICS of the ARMIES of the LIBERATION

1) THE AMERICAN TRANSPORT DEPOT

On June 22nd, at the Carentan crossroads, the military police counted 18,836 vehicles, or a total traffic of 1,100 vehicles / hour. One month later, the bridge-head was 50 km wide, 25 km deep and totalled 125,000 operational vehicles, whilst the assembly workshops in La Cambe and Isigny put together 500 jeeps and trucks per day, from huge wooden crates. Other teams "unwaterproofed" 4,217 tanks and half tracks and 3,500 pieces of artillery.

By the end of June, 137,041 vehicles were rid of their waterproofing made of cloth and putty and of other accessories, such as air exhaust pipes. Immaculate on leaving the depots, the transport vehicles were led to the Service Corps companies where they were given their divisionary emblems depending on the army unit or transport service corps (USA) to which they were to belong. The command designated two drivers per truck. The men were then instructed that both they and their vehicles should remain in the best possible condition ! For an advance to be successful (arrival of the troops or supplies at the exact time to the exact destination, in good condition), all of the vehicles had to be prepared correctly, tools and spare parts checked and spare petrol and lubricants loaded. The speed along the road was used to the maximum, in close columns in case of emergencies, thus reducing guidance staff along the way but increasing the drivers' fatigue. Whether the columns were light or spread out, the speed of the trucks was set by the slowest vehicles of the convoys, the narrow roads, bridges and bad weather.

The ordinary advance speed was an average speed of 32 km/hour, ie. real speed of 44 km/hour. The tracked vehicles travelled 240 km in 24 hours at a speed of 28 km/hour. The advance distance was always the equivalent to the speed on the speedometer, doubled when in tight columns and tripled in wide columns.

Good advance was made when :
- The group knew the itinerary and was well-guided ;
- The trucks were well-loaded with no arms or legs hanging over the sides, thus likely to cause injuries and slow down the proceedings ;
- Order was kept during fuel and meal stops of 45 minutes each, by day or by night and rest stops of 10 minutes for every hour driven ;
- Any vehicles, having broken down, were pushed clear of the roadway and forbidden from re-joining the column ;
- Liaison and first aid vehicles could overtake the column without exceeding 72 km/hour.

By the end of August, 5,958 2.5 ton trucks of the "Red Ball Express Circuit" were in working order, answering to 132 truck companies to deliver 12,432 tons per day over a period of 18 days !

The movement of an armoured division amounted to a column of 6,175 vehicles of all types or, in England, to 2,427 wagons !

The daily fuel consumption was of 500,000 litres in slow progress and sometimes reached 700,000 litres in quick progress.

COM-Z publicity, American communication zones in charge of transporting supplies throughout Continental Europe.

► *A fleet of 2.5 tons American GMCs belonging to the COM-Z, near Bricquebec.*

Amphibious DUKWs.

The LOGISTICS of the ARMIES
of the LIBERATION

General Patton :

"The 2.5 ton GMC truck is our most precious weapon".

2) AMERICAN FLEET VEHICLES INVENTORY

From the 18th July, the 3rd Army set up a transport depot in Bricquebec entitled the 514th Quartermaster Group. Loads of 8 to 10 tons were frequent on GMC trucks and the teams were stretched to the hilt, trying to transport their most precious supplies. In August, the roads of Brittany were difficult for the men of the Service Corps, who had no option but to learn to drive in the midst of the action.

Millions of tyres crushed the dust until it became so fine it got into the mechanisms of the engines, into clothes, into eyes and even into food. But nothing was impossible for the transport companies ! And the rear troops quickly lost their reputation of leading the "quiet life" to become acquainted with the stress of the combat troops, 24 hours per day, with no hot meals, nor mail and less rest. They were split up into companies of 48 GMC trucks, each of which had a 6 wheel drive and a live load of 336 tons, 48 of which were in trailers. It took 403 hours of manual labour to unload the 336 tons and 448 hours to reload, thus a total of 851 hours of manual labour (7 tons per man per 24 hours). One GMC truck (2.5 tons) could transport 125 19litre jerrycans (5 gallons) on its floor and there was space left over for flat packing !

The loading teams tended to fill the space with another layer of jerry cans, thus transporting 5 tons instead of 2.5 tons ! The ellipsoids of suspension springs were regularly checked to avoid sagging.

In August, with 37 divisions on the front, Eisenhower admitted to being faced with the following problem : transporting some 20,000 tons of daily supplies from the ports to the front, following the armies which were making major advances. "Each kilometre further doubled the difficulty for the drivers of the loaded trucks, for they then had to return to the beaches or to the ports of Cherbourg and Arromanches, in a constant toing and froing. The transporting of the equipment to lay bridges, repair roads and maintain them, of fuel for planes in the airfields which were also constantly moving, was also necessary …".

The American 2.5 ton truck was in the instrumental American victory in France in 1944.

By the end of August, the Allied vehicle fleet totalled 381,451 vehicles of all descriptions, excluding tanks and tracked vehicles. The production of maps by the Allied Headquarters, printed in colour, reached 7.5 million copies per month (1/100 000, 1/50 000, 1/25 000, 1/5 000, 1/2 500).

Normal American Vehicles

	Consumption	Fuel tank capacity	Max. speed
Dodge WC 54	30 l/100	113 l	87 km/h
AM M8 (Automatic machine gun)	31 l/100	223 l	90 km/h
HT M2 (Half Track)	95 l/100	227 l	70 km/h
H T M3	60 l/100	227 l	70 km/h
Dodge Command Car WC 56	30 l/100	113 l	85 km/h
Packard Plymouth or Ford 2 GA	15 l/100	65 l	90 km/h
White Scout car M3AI	30 l/100	114 l	90 km/h
Affut Arty autoprop M7	240 l/100	700 l	40 km/h
Affut M8 (Stuart 75 mm)	157 l/100	337 l	55 km/h
M10 AI Tank Destroyer	235 l/100	726 l	40 km/h
M12 155 mm carries	470 l/100	757 l	40 km/h
HT M13	50 l/100	265 l	70 km/h
M5 Stuart tank	118 l/100	336 l	65 km/h
M3 Stuart tank	235 l/100	700 l	40 km/h
M4 AI Tank	235 l/100	664 l	35 km/h
M4 A2 Tank	118 l/100	560 l	35 km/h
M4 A3/A4 Tank	235 l/100	659 l	42 km/h
Bulldozer Cat M3	118 l/100	340 l	15 km/h
Arty M4 Tractor	118 l/100	473 l	48 km/h
Caterpillar D7 Bulldozer	157 l/100	246 l	5 km/h
Jeep Willys/Ford 1/4 t	12 l/100	56,7 l	105 km/h
Dodge WC-11	20 l/100	94,6 l	90 km/h
Dodge WC-51	30 l/100	113,6 l	85 km/h
Truck 1.5 t Chevrolet	36,2 l/100	113,5 l	77 km/h
Dodge 6 x 6 with 4 wheeldrive	38 l/100	113,50 l	87 km/h
GMC 6 x 6 ordnance	40 l/100	115 l	72 km/h
GMC 6 x 6 352-A2	40 l/100	115 l	72 km/h
Diamond T (4 t)	94 l/100	227 l	65 km/h
Coach and Brockway (6 t)	94 l/100	227 l	65 km/h
Mack NM5	75 l/100	303 l	55 km/h
Ward La France 10 t	94 l/100	379 l	72 km/h
Coach tractor 4,5 t	73,5 l/100	227 l	70 km/h
Federal tractor 4,5 t	94 l/100	234 l	65 km/h
Diamond T 9 t	117,5 l/100	568 l	35 km/h

Under great pressure from the incessant convoys of vehicles, the roads of Normandy were repaired and maintained by the US Engineers, here in Airel to the North of St Lô.

A liaison jeep in Patton's Army and its driver.

The "Red Ball Express" passing through Mortain. Here carrying US munitions.

FUEL
LOGISTICS

The exceptional demand created by Operation Overlord, especially in terms of fuel, required specific preparation, which corresponded to 25 % of all Transatlantic crossing to the United Kingdom.

As early as the end of 1943, the Chiefs of Staff had designated Port-en-Bessin as the port capable of receiving fuel supplies for all the Allied armies, until Cherbourg was liberated.

In February 1944, a POL Headquarters was created under the command of Colonel Freeman Budford with staff from companies such as Esso, Shell, Motor-oil and Humble. The carriage chain was the responsibility of the General Supply Corps and Transport Corps, whereas the packaging of supplies into casks or jerry-cans was that of the Engineering Corps.

The vehicles of the park consumed on average :
- 35l/100 km for trucks ;
- 110l/100 km for halftracks ;
- 235l/100 km for tanks.

The demand on :
- D-Day + 14 was of 67,000 vehicles ;
- D-Day + 41 was of 183,000 vehicles ;
- D-Day + 90 was of 263,000 vehicles.

In Port-en-Bessin, which was operational as a fuel port from D-Day + 10, the tankers dropped anchor 2 miles off in an unloading zone. They were then connected to off-shore cables which ran into the coast using 15 cm tubes, which took the precious fuel to the pumping stations. The pumping stations then pumped the petrol and diesel for the American 1st Army into huge diesel tanks located in St Honorine-des-Pertes and huge petrol tanks by Mont Cauvin in Etreham and to Omaha Beach for the Navy depot.

Fuel required by the Air Forces was pumped directly to the airfields in Tour-en-Bessin (USAAF) and in Coulombs (RAF). The tanks in Etreham contained 24,000 tons, i.e. 4.8 million litres of fuel, those in St Honorine, 4 million litres (20,000 tons). The carriage was completed mostly in barrels and jerry-cans, with some 5 million litres in reserve on the bridgehead, 3 weeks after D-Day. To meet their objectives, the Allies had to ensure the arrival in Normandy of 271,158 tons of POL in the 42 days following D-Day, including fuel of 80,000 tons. Two pipeline systems were set up : **the minor and major systems.**

▲ *Port-en-Bessin. The oil pipeline crossing over the LCT which had accidentally hit the jetty.*

① THE MINOR SYSTEM

*It was the **Port-en-Bessin off-shore station**, which delivered the fuel from its pumping stations and pipelines of 15 cm in diameter in rows of 6 to the tanks in Etreham, St Honorine-des-Pertes and Colleville on the one hand. Fuel for the army (MT80), some 54,000 tons, i.e. 11 million litres in reserve, was stocked in Balleroy, with another 13 million litres stocked in air force depots.*
The fuel came from Wells in Texas, from where it was transported in numerous pipelines before reaching Massachusetts where it was loaded onto tankers. The East Coast of the USA had also numerous military industrial depots, from which goods were loaded onto merchant navy ships from New York to Connecticut.
The Jeeps came from Detroit, M1 rifles from Massachusetts, colts and machine guns from Hartford, radios from Pennsylvania, artillery shells from Illinois, K rations from Wisconsin and blood plasma from Memphis, Tennessee.

The minor fuel supplies system, operational from June 16th onwards, was to play an essential role throughout the 77 days of the Normandy Campaign. The delay in taking Cherbourg, the time required to clean up the city and make it operational again, prevented the arrival of the major Pluto system (Pipeline under the Ocean) before the 2nd half of the month of August. The limited movement in the narrow bridgehead in June and July meant that Port-en-Bessin's minor system was sufficient, with an increased debit of 2,000 tons per day instead of the 700 initially planned.
The Eastern jetty was reserved for the British, the Western jetty for the Americans. Major difficulties were encountered in bad weather to secure and link up the tankers to the off-shore connections, but generally speaking, with the willing help of French

civilians and fishermen, who transported the barrels on their small boats when the pipelines were out-of-use, the average supplies required were produced. The 786th US Engineers Petroleum Coy was operational in Port-en-Bessin on June 25th and the first tank was filled on the Mont Cauvin (Etreham) 9 days later, despite the gigantic stock of jerrycans waiting in and around the beaches.
The pipelines were then extended towards Carentan for air force gas (av-gas), towards Isigny and Montebourg (2,400 tons in stock) and later towards St. Lô (MT 80 for the army). By the end of July, instead of the 45 km of pipeline initially planned, 115 km were laid from Port-en-Bessin, with some 30 million litres stocked in tanks, as opposed to the 11 million expected. By the end of July, the minor system produced 2.4 million litres per day, whilst Bradley's army alone required 1.8 million litres of fuel. By mid-September, it produced 3.6 million litres per day for the armies as they approached the Rhine before Le Havre, and later Boulogne, picked up the relay. Fuel, "the red blood of war", piped from Port-en-Bessin through the minor system was always in sufficient quantities for the 2 million men and their 500,000 vehicles, which made up the bridgehead in liberated Normandy.
By the end of August, the major system came in addition to the minor system from Cherbourg with 4 million litres per day, without ever supplanting Port-en-Bessin, where the Royal Engineers had created two landing lines for ships at sea, by pontoons, 6 anchor points for tankers with 6 off-shore connections (tombolas), a zone of reservoirs and MT80 petrol pumps (9,800 tons in reserve) and av-gas (2,000 tons) as well as 3 pipelines to BLAY where 1,400 tons could be stocked.
Another pipeline led to the airfield in Coulombs (80 tons per hour when necessary). The stocks in Balleroy, 40 km away, could hold 10.8 million litres and were supplied by 4 pipelines and 6 pumps from Port-en-Bessin.

One of the MT80 Petrol Tanks on Mount Cauvin.

Minor system fuel pumping on the Mount Cauvin (Etreham).

Background image : minor system pipeline in Port-en-Bessin

FUEL
LOGISTICS

② THE MAJOR SYSTEM

This was to be the revolution of the summer of 1944 in terms of fuel supplies : **PLUTO** (Pipeline under the Ocean), also known as the "Red Blood Express" to recall the express road transport network "Red Ball Express". This was History's first ever oil pipeline, dating from 1942 and conceived by Admiral Lord Louis Mountbatten. There were 2 different underwater oil pipeline systems, which stretched from Sandown on the Isle of Wight to Querqueville, to the West of Cherbourg. The first line was set up on the 13th August 1944 and the 2nd on August 21st. The means were then adapted to the two types of pipeline.

A - HAMEL

Hamel was composed of the initials of the names of the engineers Hammick (of the Irak Petroleum Company) and Ellis (of the Burma Oil Company). Hamel was a flexible and relatively light tube, 7.6 cm in diameter, which was rolled around a floating drum, itself 15 cm in diameter and 27 m long, containing, just like a huge spool, 112 km of oil pipeline tubing. 6 floating drums were built, which could unroll six pipelines simultaneously, dragged by tugs from the Isle of Wight to Cherbourg in one go. The weight of each drum when loaded was of 1,600 tons, ie. that of a destroyer. Their code name was HMS Conundrum, thus associated with one of Her Majesty's vessels and its tug.

Pipeline
under the ocean

◄ Floating spool
by a high sea
the HAMEL
pipeline.

Floating spool for 112 km
of HAMEL type pipeline.

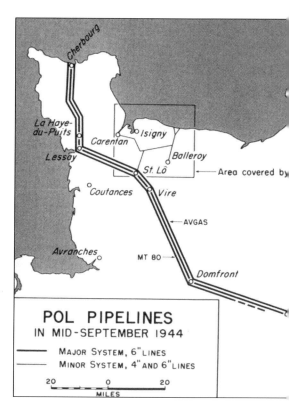

POL PIPELINES
IN MID-SEPTEMBER 1944

—— MAJOR SYSTEM, 6" LINES
—— MINOR SYSTEM, 4" AND 6" LINES

PLUTO

NORMANDY 1944

B - HAIS

Heavier than the Hamel, the HAIS was an oil pipeline, laid by a special ship at the centre of which was the pipe drum, known as HMS Holfast. Two other cable ships were built. This system which owed its name to the engineer Hartley of the Anglo-Iranian Oil Company and to Siemens, the manufacturer of the pipeline, was the first to reach Querqueville in mid-August 1944. The unloading of tankers was, up until then, carried out by connections made to pipelines which ran across the length and breadth of Normandy in the wake of the armies.

PLUTO was a 100 % British project of 10 underwater tubes, each of 7.6 cm in diameter, covering 100 km, supplying 300 tons of fuel per day. A system of motorpumps re-injected and dispatched the petrol into pipes of 15 cm in diameter towards Saint Lô, Laval and Etampes at the end of August. Each pipe could transport up to 1,825 tons per day. From July onwards, a fuel stock zone was created to the South of Querqueville. There were 38 tanks, each able to contain 10,000 tons (a capacity of 66 million litres), interconnected, spread out and camouflaged along the hillside. The pumping relay stations were spread from Querqueville to la Haye-du-Puits, Coutances, Avranches, Fougères, Rennes, Laval (D-Day + 41) then to Craon and Chateaubriand (D-Day + 46), totalling 83 pumping stations.

P ipe
L ine
U nder
T he
O cean.

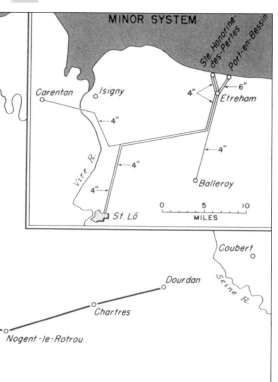

*HMS Persephone :
central spool
for unloading HAIS type pipeline.* ▲

FUEL
LOGISTICS

The filling of 20 litre jerrycans from US Transportation Corps trucks in a POL Depot.

Both the oil pipeline systems, the minor and major systems, extended over 8,864 km in September, producing 586,000 tons or 10.7 million litres in total capacity. This was a huge headache for the planners, who had to anticipate the troops' advance, the enemy's reaction, imagine the weather conditions as well as calculating the consumption rate of the vehicles and planes … with no room for errors !

It was, therefore, always wise to count in surplus, whilst being fully aware of which areas were in need of priority supplies. At this point in the campaign, the 1st American Army alone required 1.8 million litres per day. The 1st and 3rd American Armies needed 4 million litres per day during phases of major advancing. If we are to add to this the 1st and 2nd British and Canadian Armies, they used up over 8 million litres of MT80 petrol per day, with a reserve stock for 12 days (100 million litres).

The major and minor fuel supply systems required 7,700 Allied soldiers and approximately 1,500 voluntary prisoners of war. To these men were added 3 battalions of military police whose job it was to protect the huge deployment of oil pipelines, often sabotaged, or simply pierced by some civilians for their personal usage, who then scampered, leaving the pipes to leak ! And if they hadn't chosen the wrong pipeline in the first place, as the supplies were carried through 3 parallel pipelines : one for avgas and 2 MT80 (car).

The speed of the Allied offensive after the 24th August meant that the Armies were advancing quicker than the laying of the pipelines. They reached Alençon, from where shuttles of road tankers began following the Allied vehicles, with a considerable distance to cover (return). This was the start of the supply crisis in the West at the time of the liberation of Paris, where 6,000 trucks were insufficient to catch up on "the time lost due to the too speedy advance !".

At the beginning of September, the Allies discovered the true tyranny of logistics on which all operational plans depend. In Normandy, before the 24th August, an armoured division used 4 tons of munitions for 1 ton of fuel per day. After the 25th August, these proportions were reversed (4 tons of fuel for 1 ton of munitions per day).

Piles of 20 litre jerrycans which were named after the German containers copied by the Allies as early as 1942.

③ AVIATION FUEL (AVGAS)

In August 1944, there were 39 Allied airfields in Lower-Normandy, operated by the Anglo-Canadians of the 2nd TAF (Tactical Air Force, RAF) and the 9th USAAF and 19th Air Corps. Each of these advanced airfields was used by 60 fighter bombers, using 550 litres of fuel per hour and completing several missions per day !

From D-Day until June 23rd (D + 17), only a little over 2.3 million tons of avgas had been used (bad weather), whereas at the beginning of August, 1 million tons of avgas were used every day !

The aviation fuel came from the minor system in Port-en-Bessin where it was stocked in huge, covered, pre-fabricated tanks called "MARENGs", 36 tanks with a capacity of 30,000 litres to 137,000 litres. The western loading points took fuel to the 9th US AAF, the eastern points to the 2nd TAF (RAF).

The fuel was transported for a long time in containers and by tanker lorries until the pipelines reached Coulombs (RAF), Isigny and Balleroy (USAAF). The stocks were 5 to 1 and, at the beginning of August, almost 10 million litres were held in reserve in Port-en-Bessin, which had become France's main fuel port, after the collapse of German resistance in the West. The Allied advance was much faster than the laying of the pipeline and the trains were no longer sufficient to supply the airfields, which, following the armies, were also advancing, on a circuit of 1,300 km by the 1st September from Port-en-Bessin. The Cherbourg pipeline (PLUTO) was finally to reach Chartres by the end of September to end in Châlons-sur-Marne in January 1945.

The permanent and regular road supply was, however, more efficient than the pipelines, which were often needing repaired for various reasons.

▲ *Supplying fuel for P47s of the 9th USAAF in Cartigny-l'Epinay.*

◀ *An American supplies column for the Red Blood Express Advanced airfields.*

EXAMPLE OF THE CONVOYS FOR THE 9TH US ARMY AIR FORCE
Transport by the tanker lorries and In jerrycans from Port en Bessin (minor system) :

JULY :	6,574,000 litres
SEPTEMBER :	34,875,000 litres
DECEMBER :	45,000,000 litres

ALLIED TRANSPORT LOGISTICS

In the Overlord plan, from D + 50 (26ᵗʰ July), it was planned that the road transport needs would be superior to those of the transport of army staff and their equipment. It was at this point, that the communications headquarters, called COM-Z or "Communication Zone" came into the picture with, at its disposal, a park of some 5,000 lorries and service vehicles. COM-Z's role was to establish a liaison between the supply depots by ensuring connection pathways, clearing and maintaining the roads, then the railways, increasing the capacity of the various ports and finally ensuring the movements of prisoners of war and civilians.

If shooting broke out, a special emergency delivery system was set up, the "Red Ball Express", which was composed of loads of 1,000 tons of supplies, already waiting in trucks on permanent alert and checked every day. Another emergency transport system was the "Green Light", which replaced essential cargoes lost at sea or in the air.

For every truck, a load is ready awaiting transport to the front. ▼

▲ *In Normandy : American Class I (food) depots. The piles of crates were carefully covered by waterproof sheets.*

① THE DEPOTS

The depots, in the American sector, were set up from Omaha and Utah beaches until Cherbourg reached equivalent productivity around the 20th August. Omaha was an excellent example of a landing operation from the rows of ships neatly in line, unloaded by the amphibious DUKWs and the LSTs grounded along the 7.5 km beach to the wide exit roads, so toughly fought over on D-Day. These roads were impeccably rebuilt, cleared and maintained by the engineers.

Nothing could be seen of the disaster zone left behind by D-Day. 11,000 men and 2,000 vehicles crossed Omaha every day with some 9,000 tons of supplies in July and August (95 % of Overlord's logistics' plan). On Utah beach, 7,500 men and 800 vehicles transporting some 5,500 tons of supplies on average per day left the long beach (8 km) via the only too rare roadways, which emerged from the flooded zones (97 % of the plan). D-Day was over as was the storm, which had slowed the landing of supplies by 2/3 , to such an extent that Ike himself, at this point, considered it as "a drop in the ocean of supplies rolling onto the Normandy

◀ *The Montebourg Depot of the US Normandy Base Section.*

coast". From this point onwards, the depots were no longer hidden in the hedgerows but set up in open fields, in piles with no camouflage, as the risks of an enemy air attack had been become so minor.

The few "hard" depots were in Cherbourg, in the buildings of the "Amiot" factory or in the main hanger of the French aeronaval in Ecausseville, which had been transformed into "ordnance maintenance shop".

◀ *Omaha Beach. A row of LSTs neatly lined up, unloaded by DUKWs and GMCs.*

The ALLIED
TRANSPORT LOGISTICS

The depot zone for the secondary ports of Isigny, Carentan and Grandcamp was set up in Trévières. The Omaha depot zone was in Formigny and in Surrain and the Utah depot around Chef-du-Pont. But in the eye of an untrained observer, it seemed, at the time, that almost every field was used by the Supply Corps or some other auxiliary body. On occasions, the Luftwaffe showed some resistance as in Formigny on July 15th where, besides human losses, 2,000 tons of munitions went up in smoke. As a result, the transport vehicles were parked some distance from the depots. The first park of the US Transport Corps was thus set up in Briquebec on July 5th (the depot zone was in Chef-du-Pont), with a traffic flow at the crossroads in St Sauveur-le-Vicomte, reaching 1,000 vehicles per hour. In Formigny, it reached over 1,800 vehicles per hour. Between Carentan and Isigny, the bridges over the Vey and the Vire had to support a traffic flow of 14,434 vehicles from 6 am to 9 pm on July 18th. Roundabouts were built, the military police directed traffic at all junctions, Bailey bridges were built to help with the increasing frequency of traffic, to such an extent that the Normans, caught up in this whirlwind of traffic, began to regret the slower pace of "before D-Day". On one-way roads between St Mère-Eglise and Isigny, at the beginning of July, some 30,000 tons of supplies per day were transported without any Luftwaffe or artillery interference. On July 25th, immediately following the American breakthrough to the West of St Lô, operation COBRA, the aim of which was to give depth to the narrow American bridgehead under the command of General Lee, in charge of COM-Z, set up base in the chateaux of Pont-Rilly and of Servigny in Valognes. These two bases became the headquarters of the COM-Z advanced scale, and of the COM-Z in general at the beginning of August when Patton's 3rd Army crossed the Cotentin peninsula heading for Brittany. By this point in the Landings, 815,000 GIs, 640,000 British and Commonwealth soldiers were in Normandy with 36 divisions. In accordance with the Overlord plan (to spread out into Brittany, capture ports, then move East to reach the Seine with the support from the Loire, creating an encirclement around Normandy), the Americans were given priority in the distribution of fuel supplies to ensure the success of their mission ; and General Eisenhower, as a result of this, was met by severe criticism from Winston Churchill.
According to the Germans, who had considerable experience in this field : "the lightening war" "Blitzkrieg" was the tactician's paradice, but the general administrator's hell".
It was thus, in this "lightening war", led by Patton's "Lucky forward" 3rd Army, where the most optimistic previsions were surpassed, that the highest level of fuel consumption and the dangerously lowest supplies level were recorded (on August 6th, Bradley's 1st US Army had 11 days' supplies ahead whereas Patton's 3rd Army at best had only 1 !).
To enable Patton to move to encircle the Norman front, between the Seine, the Orne and the Loire rivers, General Lee excelled to supply him 13,250 tons of supplies per day in comparison to Bradley's 6,144 from August 7th to August 16th. But the Americans' basic arms supplies, used in July in hedgerow battles, had yet to reach the authorized level (grenades, BAR, 60MM Shells, bazookas and their munitions).
Patton's 3rd Army lacked the stocks of Bradley's 1st Army who, spoilt during the Landings, had since, in fear of shortages, constituted its own illegal stocks totally unknown to the military administration. In the 70 days of the campaign, the Americans lost 2,400, BAR's, 1,750 jeeps, 908 Sherman tanks, 1,500 mortars and 2,000 planes ! The War Department had planned for a 7% loss in equipment to be replaced. But Bradley's 1st Army alone, from D-Day to July 30th, beat all statistics reaching a rate of 29% losses, especially in Sherman tanks, where reserves were exhausted by the end of August.
In August, the rationing of daily artillery munitions was required in the 1st Army, as 851,000 105 mm shells had been used in July. The road convoys were attributed to Patton's army, the army which legitimately required the most supplies, and the ships could no longer be unloaded at the same speed due to a lack of lorries. The situation was identical in the depots which were full to the brim with equipment and materials stocked in fields, due to the lack of ports and transport, thus contradicting the Transport Corps' saying which went "if you've something to transport, the TC will do it !".

▲ A transport convoy of American tanks belonging to Patton's Army passes through Avranches, which is the world's busiest town in terms of traffic in August 1944.

A - THE NORMANDY BASE SECTION

This section was in charge of controlling deliveries in the zone to the North of St Lô. Its logistics were those of the COM-Z, from the 7th August onwards, with 132 transport companies, each having 45 trucks, forming an impressive fleet of 5,958 GMCs ! The Normandy Supply Base stretched over three sites from Cherbourg – Utah – Omaha. The base was split into 6 Normandy Base Sections, which, in turn, were split into districts. The Cherbourg Base Section was opened on 6th July 1944 and operated until February 1945. This section was responsible for the rail and road convoys in transit through Cherbourg and 123,000 men were based at these headquarters. General Lee's COM-Z staff totalled 646,000 men on the continent in October 1944. Each of the American sites had a particular specificity : 163,000 vehicles and 279,000 men landed on Utah Beach, 123,000 vehicles and 512,000 men on Omaha, with the remaining logistics in Cherbourg : railway materials, coal, general supplies, mechanical parts of all types.

All of these supplies were handled by the greatly favoured transport corps with General Lee playing a major role. He did, indeed, abuse his power, both politically and practically, by authorizing one type of priority supplies to his mates, in charge of such and such a corps or by providing himself in Valognes with such luxurious comfort and Eisenhower and Patton, green with envy were not long in telling him what they thought of logistics for the American Army appointed by General Marshall, Chief of Staff of the American Army, Lee had set himself up in pompous comfort using up an extravagant quantity of supplies and camps, which were sadly lacking elsewhere. In September, he had his private train, that had caused great jealousy before the invasion, brought to Normandy. On August 30th, when he left Valognes for Paris, he gave priority to the transfer of his COM-Z over 300 km at the peak of the fuel crisis ! He set up his headquarters in the main hotels along the major boulevards and made himself a good number of enemies when the troops discovered that the COM-Z boasted its comfort brazenly, making the most of Paris and its charms at the height of war.

A moment's relaxation by a US Depot canteen truck.

ALLIED
TRANSPORT LOGISTICS

B - AMERICAN ENGINEERING IN LOGISTICS

The American Engineering Corps was responsible, from the early hours of D-Day onwards, for the creation of the advanced depot zones directly on the beaches. Then, like the British Engineering Corps, they built the intermediary bases for food rations and the army depots with munitions, magazines, vehicles, fleets, assembly, maintenance and repair workshops, etc.

In the 6 weeks following D-Day, 1 million m² of sheltered stock depots had been completed and 3 million m2 of open-air depots. Stockage space for 130,000 tons of munitions was spread over 400 km of roads and pathways. The maintenance of communication routes was a priority, with one engineering regiment capable of building 15 km of roadway per day and of ensuring the maintenance of a further 200 km. By June 30th, 5 regiments were responsible for consolidating the bridgehead along with 2 "civil" engineering companies. Later, another 5 general engineering regiments joined these efforts along with 3 truck companies and a battalion of civil engineers to excavate quarries (gravel, stones), build roads, make cement, lay Bailey bridges and transport some 47,500 tons of various materials for road repair work. Beside, with 75 % of the French railroads destroyed, the engineers had their work cut out for them.

Landing ports ▶

Cherbourg : Querqueville Quayside, 1 ; Naval Arsenal, 2.

Cherbourg : amphibious DUKW landing zones behind the ferry terminal.
▼

Unloading of an English heavy MATADOR truck belonging to the RAF in the pebbles on Omaha Beach. ▶

ALLIED
TRANSPORT LOGISTICS

② "THE TRANSPORTATION CORPS"

The role of the transportation corps was to "ensure all transport successfully in collaboration with port traffic, the intermediary depots and to maintain the lines of communication open by regulating traffic frequency" (General Clarence Burpee). Their theoretical means were composed of 240 transport companies, each with 48 vehicles and 2 drivers per vehicle ensuring a round-the-clock transport provision ! American railroad transport was possible from D + 41 onwards and was entrusted to 2 rail workshop battalions and 2 operational battalions, who had at their disposal by D + 65, 900 locomotives and 100,000 wagons. The 11th Carriage Command was responsible for their repair and maintenance with 7,700 men in 4 carriage battalions and 5 DUKW (250) companies. The 1055th Engineers Carriage Repair Group began the rehabilitation of the railway station in Carentan as early as June 17th (it had been liberated on June 13th). Then, efforts were moved to Lison (25th June) and later, in July, to Cherbourg. Therefore, the first railroad to be rebuilt was opened on July 11th operating in the Cherbourg, Lison, Carentan triangle. The first train to use the line was composed of the 729th railroad Operational Battalion and served Cherbourg, Barfleur, St. Sauveur-le-Vicomte, St Vaast-la-Hougue, Carentan and Lison. It was sponsored by the New York Railroad Company

from Hartford, Connecticut. The 707th Engineers Battalion landed on July 7th by LSTs on Utah beach with the first Diesel locomotive ever in France (25 tons) and 10 wagons, as forerunners. Two weeks later, the "sea trains" Texas and Lakehurst delivered the first of the 200 locomotives they were to bring across the Atlantic to Cherbourg. At this point, the double Cherbourg, Lison, Valognes, Carentan railroad was extended to include Folligny, Avranches, Dol, Rennes, St Hilaire and Mayennne (August 12th). The railroads were economical, provided good frequency, but required a lot of equipment and bridges.

When the first train reached Le Mans after leaving Cherbourg, at the time of the Battle for Falaise, it had crossed 97 Bailey bridges recently built by the engineers to replace the rail bridges, which had been a systematical target of the Allied bombers over the 3 previous months.

The first American train, from Le Mans to Paris, entered Batignolles station on the 30th August 1944. Over 5,000 prisoners of war were employed on the maintenance of the railways with a wide use of German railroad equipment, which the Allies had salvaged. The SNCF only recovered its network once the 13,000 American soldiers from the Rail Carriage and Engineering Units had completed their work in April 1945 !

▼ *US Transportation Corps locomotives.*

A US medical train in the ferry terminal in Cherbourg. ▶

ALLIED TRANSPORT LOGISTICS

Red Ball Express emblem (Transportation Corps). ▶

A - THE RED BALL EXPRESS (M.T.C.)

The Red Ball Express was the answer to the emergency call to the army's transport corps in an attempt to resolve a logistics' crisis for which the High Command had not planned.

On 40 occasions in June and July in the United Kingdom, the green and red emergency lights for certain types of supplies had lit up.

"Green light" and "Red Ball" replied by parachuting supplies of medicine (penicillin) or munitions (105 mm) or both to isolated troops or to those in need. By the end of July, 6,600 tons had been thus delivered by air (C47 Dakota or Skytrain).

The encircling of two German armies in Normandy by Patton's army (3rd US Army) led the 8th and 12th US Corps to Orleans and to Mantes across the Seine, after the Norman loop net had closed in on the German 5th and 7th Armies, partially defeated. From this point onwards, General Bradley's 12th American Army group headed to the North-East of Paris, at first making fast progress (end of August), later to be slowed down because of the delivery of supplies (beginning of September). Fieldmarshal Montgomery's 21st British Army group advanced on Le Havre, Saint-Valery, Dieppe and then Boulogne at the beginning of September, with shorter distances to cover from the rear bases than his American colleague. This was the beginning of the critical phase in logistics for the Allies, who where faced with difficult choices : to support Patton's objective of the German border or to support the Anglo-Canadian targets of the V1 bases and the ports ?

Suddenly stretched to their limits in the space of a few days at the end of August, from Cherbourg to Brest and from Omaha/Arromanches to Paris/Melun, the Anglo-American communication lines were no longer able to meet with the demand placed upon them. The bottleneck in Avranches was the world's busiest highway in mid-August of 1944.

On August 25th, in order to compensate this critical deficit in the advanced zones, the Red Ball plan (Motorized Transportation Corps) was launched with a gigantic one-way road transport system over a long distance (700 km) from the advanced divisionary zones to the rear bases in Normandy. This rapid and unexpected advance to the East in a new lightning war forced General LEE's COM-Z to place, as a matter of urgency, 100,000 tons of supplies and 20 million litres of fuel into the Chartres, La Loupe, Dreux triangle before September 1st, with 20% transported by rail and 82,000 tons by road !

US Transmissions technicians controlling COM-Z radio equipment.

Officers of the American Service of Supplies, in August 1944.

Thus the Red Ball Express was born ! Those directly responsible in COM-Z Headquarters were Colonel Loren AYERS, Head of the Motor Transport System and Major Gordon GRAVELLE with 141 GMC truck companies from the advanced section of which 132 (6,000 trucks) were immediately available.

Red Ball and its daily tonnage target. ▶

ALLIED
TRANSPORT LOGISTICS

Red Ball fuel convoy, controlled
by the military police.

◄ The Red Ball Express route was best
avoided !

Fleet of 2.5 tons American trucks on the Cotentin
peninsula (Montebourg and Bricquebec).

TRUCK ROUTES

LEGEND

RED BALL HIGHWAY
WHITE BALL HIGHWAY
GREEN DIAMOND HIGHWAY
A B C HIGHWAY

SCALE-IN-MILES

P·O·L
IN
ETO
APRIL 25, 1945

BEING USED
ABANDONED

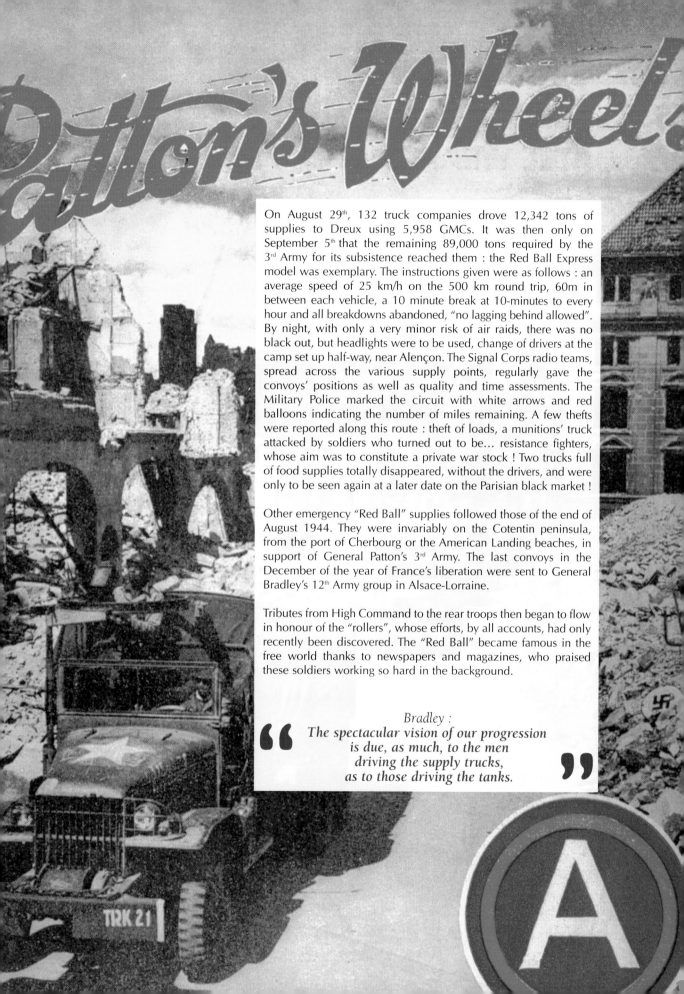

On August 29th, 132 truck companies drove 12,342 tons of supplies to Dreux using 5,958 GMCs. It was then only on September 5th that the remaining 89,000 tons required by the 3rd Army for its subsistence reached them : the Red Ball Express model was exemplary. The instructions given were as follows : an average speed of 25 km/h on the 500 km round trip, 60m in between each vehicle, a 10 minute break at 10-minutes to every hour and all breakdowns abandoned, "no lagging behind allowed". By night, with only a very minor risk of air raids, there was no black out, but headlights were to be used, change of drivers at the camp set up half-way, near Alençon. The Signal Corps radio teams, spread across the various supply points, regularly gave the convoys' positions as well as quality and time assessments. The Military Police marked the circuit with white arrows and red balloons indicating the number of miles remaining. A few thefts were reported along this route : theft of loads, a munitions' truck attacked by soldiers who turned out to be… resistance fighters, whose aim was to constitute a private war stock ! Two trucks full of food supplies totally disappeared, without the drivers, and were only to be seen again at a later date on the Parisian black market !

Other emergency "Red Ball" supplies followed those of the end of August 1944. They were invariably on the Cotentin peninsula, from the port of Cherbourg or the American Landing beaches, in support of General Patton's 3rd Army. The last convoys in the December of the year of France's liberation were sent to General Bradley's 12th Army group in Alsace-Lorraine.

Tributes from High Command to the rear troops then began to flow in honour of the "rollers", whose efforts, by all accounts, had only recently been discovered. The "Red Ball" became famous in the free world thanks to newspapers and magazines, who praised these soldiers working so hard in the background.

> *Bradley :*
> **The spectacular vision of our progression is due, as much, to the men driving the supply trucks, as to those driving the tanks.**

ALLIED
TRANSPORT LOGISTICS

Patton :
" *The prospect of a crushing victory has made those, upon whose shoulders supplies and maintenance lie, accomplish superhuman feats : it is as a result of their determination to beat the difficulties encountered during these surprising and almost unbelievable days, that, at no time whatsoever, the speed of our advance was slowed by a lack of vital supplies.* "

Eisenhower :
" *Given the ban on Le Havre and the other Breton ports, still under the occupation, and the necessity to support so long and fast an advance solely from Norman bases, only a miracle, resulting from the hard labour and magnificent resourcefulness of the Supply Corps, could have led our armoured columns so far forward. Without these men, the irresistible victory, which was to liberate France, would not have been possible.* "

(Le Havre fell to the 1ˢᵗ British Corps on September 12ᵗʰ and became the main American port one month later. Brest fell on September 17ᵗʰ but, too far from the eastern offensive, was never used as a logistics supply port).

Besides the Red Ball, the American trains loaded in Cherbourg, ran East in close convoys, defying all basic safety regulations. 900 steam and diesel engines with 100,000 wagons replaced 60 % of the French rail fleet which was paralysed. Loading remained the main problem with the railroads as well as the maintenance of the provisional civil engineering structures. Bradley even felt sorry for his colleague Von Rundstedt, who had undergone much worse ! It was essentially the Red Ball loop which enabled, 80 % of the time, the vital supplies to reach Patton's troops, due to the regularity and efficiency of the system. In Verdun, at the beginning of September, only 70 km from the Saar, Patton ran out of petrol and raged : "Good God, Brad, just give me 2 million litres and I'll have you settled in Germany in 2 days' time". It would have been easier to ask for the moon ! Verdun is 550 km from Cherbourg and the Red Ball was bled to the last drop with 2,500 trucks needing repairs from August 25ᵗʰ onwards, i.e. 800 trucks to repair per week ! It was the GMCs' belonging to the DCA or artillery units which were taken here and there as a provisional loan. 790 trucks were thus "collected" in addition to the 5,900 initial vehicles, which, in 3 weeks (25ᵗʰ August – 15ᵗʰ September), made the record of delivering 135,000 tons of supplies to Patton's army, in a crazy rotation process ; with an anecdote from those times "if you come by a Red Ball convoy, don't try to clear the road, just climb the nearest tree !".

Ingenious British Bailey bridges were the precious tools of victory.
▼

Patton's problem, in September, remained fuel from the major system whose pipeline ended in Alençon. The remaining 300 km had to be travelled by truck, which, from this point onwards, became the American army's most precious weapon.

Patton was furious because Monty had all the fuel he needed to pursue his advance in Belgium and to the ports, as Churchill had managed to gain priority from Eisenhower to capture the V1 bases, from which cruise missiles were continuing to target London. Patton could not stand this rationing and demanded that fuel transport be given priority over munitions and even foodstuff. He claimed : "My men can eat their belts. But I want my fuel !". On this circuit, which required 5 days to complete, 1 truck of petrol was required to deliver 15 to the front, from Alençon to Verdun. The average loading time of a convoy with jerrycans was of 12 hours !

This logistics crisis due to the too rapid extension of the front could have halted the Allies in their advance on Germany. (Patton : "Don't give a damn about Hodges" and Monty : "I will win this bloody war if only this engine will start again !"). In September, 85 % of supplies delivered to Patton's 3rd Army were fuel supplies, but this was still not sufficient for operations to be led in the East.

COBRA, the American breakthrough so brilliantly begun in St Lô on July 25th, had to be spaced out because of the Siegfried Line. After a month and a half of mobile war, it was to become, as it also had in June, a static war. The men were exhausted and their equipment worn out. The 3rd Army had no more replacement uniforms and 80 % of what was replaced was done so using second-hand materials. There was no time to revise the armoured cars as advised in the technical manuals : "Keep going, keep going ! You'll be serviced later". Only 35% of the armoured division fleets were still operational, dry or mechanical breakdowns gave the desolate image of roads covered in broken down vehicles over a distance of 300 km. Tank engines could not keep up the pace, their replacements too infrequent, new tracks and spare parts were lacking, not forgetting the unavoidable delivery errors and omissions difficult to erase 500 km from the supply depots in Normandy ! But the Allies were optimistical, victory was just around the corner, if only the supplies could follow ! On the 11th September 1944, the Allies landed 2.3 million men with 465,000 vehicles (49 divisions and services). In the summer of 1944, the Germans, on all fronts, lost 1,200,000 men, 500,000 of whom died in France and 100,000 blocked in coastline forts, whereas, for the same period of time, the Allies lost 225,000 human lives (killed, injured, missings). The remedy to this logistical "dead end" caused by the extension of the communications ' lines was to be heaven sent.

◀ A tank transported by the RASC passing through Rouen at the end of August 1944.

ALLIED
TRANSPORT LOGISTICS

B - AIRBORNE LOGISTICS WAS TO BE THE SOLUTION

At the end of August 1944, given the absence of foreseeable future air assaults, the US Air Tactical Transport Command and the 46th RAF Transport Group jointly delivered 2,000 tons of supplies per day. These food supplies were mainly for the Parisians, who were starving and airborne deliveries spared road convoys over the 270 km from Cherbourg to Paris, with the following message on the lead trucks "priority foodstuff for Paris". From bases in England, flights continued without interruption from August 25th to September 3rd with some 37,429 tons delivered to Paris via the "Le Bourget" Airport, which had only just been liberated. Taking the lead over England, where the Arnhem airlift was being planned, Cherbourg became the first base for the transport of Class I supplies (food) for 20 days. The US Air Engineers built the airfield in Querqueville for the specific transport of supplies into the capital. A 1,600m runway, covered with articulated take-off plates (PSP), was built in 14 hours by the 342nd General Engineers Service, for a fleet of 220 C47 Dakotas supplied directly from the avgas tanks in Querqueville. They belonged to the 31st Transport Group of the 9th US Air Force, 302nd wing. 5,000 men worked on this emergency base, which received 3,500 tons of engineering equipment in order to build it. 40,000 tons of foodstuff and medicine for the civilian population was taken to Paris, thus allowing the truck companies to be sent as military back-up to the Red Ball Express, the largest truck formation in the world !

▲ *A priority convoy of foodstuff for Paris.*

▲ *An American ….. belonging to the Air Engineers.*

Then from A21C airfield in St Laurent-sur-Mer and A22C in St Pierre-du-Mont, 1,000 tons per day were delivered to Patton's 3rd Army, essentially fuel "just enough to fill our Zippos" he complained ! This was indeed the case until September 15th. The summer air shuttle between Omaha and England ended on this date, whereas the C47 Dakotas were remobilised in preparation for imminent air operations. The two A21C and A22C airfields with the 302nd Transport Group convoyed 239,000 passengers and were responsible for evacuating 171,000 injured and sick. This group alone brought 82,000 tons of freight to Normandy amongst which : medicine, covers, radio equipment, plane engines, pumps, tyres (40,000), rain equipment, Bangalores, pyrotechnical components, cigarettes and fuel in 200 litres containers of avgas.

*American Dakota on the airfield
...erre du Mont takes part in US supplies.*

*A section of American nurses
in a C47 Dakota en route
for France.*

In August, COM-Z (road logistics) accepted the handling and delivery of supplies for the airfields, which, up until then were dealt with by the air forces. However, the field of activity was limited to within a 70 km radius from the depot bases, freight airfields and railroad terminals. If the airfield was closer, it was the air force which dealt with supplies. The air force's specific needs increased from 20 % to 30 % in terms of the replacement of planes between June and July. Carrying 3 or 4 operations per day from the Norman bases, the engines tired quickly, especially due to corrosion caused by the dust, despite the filters. This dust was also responsible for an increase in the number of ground accidents during plane movements, landings, taxiing, munitions. Additional single use reservoirs, bombs and rockets also had to be transported to the planes. From 55,000 tons of bombs used during May 1944 by the 8th and 9th US Army Air Forces alone, the evolution of events took this figure, dating from before Overlord, to 118,000 tons in March 1945 for the same army units. At the end of further airborne operations during the autumn of 1944, (1st Airborne Army, 18th Us Airborne Corps, 82nd, 101st and 17th Airborne Divisions, 1st British Airborne Division, 9th US "Troop Carrier", 46th and 38th RAF Transport Groups), the bombers transformed into cargo planes carried twice as much freight as the DC-3's especially the B24 Liberators specialized in transporting fuel for the effort required by the Allied advance. They needed hard runways, which had to be reopened as soon as possible (Creil, Beauvais, Le Bourget, Lille, Reims). But the world's largest army could not be stretched indefinitely and it was indeed in England, in order to load the planes for France, that the trucks were sadly lacking ! Under the command of the CATOR (Combined Air Transport Operations Room), the 302nd Wing and the B24s of the 8th Air Force took part in providing supplies of fuel to the Allies on the border of the Reich with almost 45,000 tons delivered by air from England in September 1944. This was an additional task which became permanent due to the rapid development of military operations, up until the new pipelines arrived in Boulogne in October (4,5 million litres per day) and in Antwerp in January 1945 with a total of 28,350,000 litres per day at the beginning of 1945 !

SMT is laid out to cover the runways in Norman airfields.

ALLIED
TRANSPORT LOGISTICS

A22C Airfield in St Pierre du Mont. Hoc Point can be seen in the top left hand corner (to the West).

◀ The American blood bank.

On an airfield,
a fleet of reserve MKIX SPITFIRES
and RAF aeronautical stocks.
▼

The American air bridge in Querqueville-Cherbourg.

On board a C47, these 155mm shells are provided in emergency.

Land, air and sea, those were the three arms that led to victory in Normandy after the collapse of the Atlantic Wall. Land-air-sea were also the three vectors of the Allied Forces' logistics in the liberation of western Europe. Not forgetting the operations led by the tactical transport groups : 1.600 gliders, 600 DUKWs and 300 LCMs landed in Le Havre for the crossing of the River Meuse and the Rhine, 650 Bailey bridges, 1,000 km of railroad… such equipment was supplied as a result of the necessity to meet with the needs of the tactical military operations as quick as possible. This fantastic organization of supplies for the 4 Allied armies was consolidated in January 1945 by the abandoning of the beaches and ports in Normandy in favour of those in Belgium, Holland and Northern Germany, and this was much to the benefit of 7 armies and 5 million men.

Montgomery's 21st group of armies :
 - CRERAR's 1st Canadian Army ; - DEMPSEY's 2nd British Army
Bradley's 12th group of US Armies :
 - HODGES' 1st US Army ; - PATTON's 3rd Army ; - SIMPSON's 9th Army.
Dever's 6th group of US Armies :
 - PATCH's 7th Army ; - De Lattre de Tassigny's 1st French Army.
The superb creativity of the British Engineering Corps was the key to the Allies' logistics with methods clearly adapted to the necessities of war : Mr Bailey's bridges, the PLUTO pipeline and the Mulberries (artificial ports), Lord Mounbatten's idea.

❸ THE MULBERRY HARBOURS AND THE BEACHES

"If we do not have the ports to land the supplies for the invasion forces, then we shall have to take them with us !" (Admiral Mountbatten, 1942). Given the uncertainty of the Allies in capturing Cherbourg, St Malo and Brest in sufficient time and in good condition, the Mulberry plan was programmed in total secrecy, even in its building, until it was completed in June 1944 and set it place on D + 12.

On 2 sites, 15 km apart, 200 high sea tugs were required to tow the components of this gigantic cubic game, like some kind of ingenious Meccano game, across the Channel : 113 Blockships, 49 communication Phoenix, 23 floating quay heads or points and 6 floating delivery roads. Tanks, cranes, bulldozers, trucks, jeeps and other ambulances for the 2nd British Army and 1st Canadian Army were landed in Arromanches and for the 1st US Army on Omaha Beach. All of the above blocks were protected by a Gooseberry or lines of old ships scuttled to act as wave breakers, often after having journeyed themselves across the Channel. 74 of these ships were sunk as outer sea walls. The implantation of the project was successfully led by 240 British industrial companies with approximately 15,000 workers. The construction of 20 replacement Phoenix elements in March 1944 was to extend the planned transporting from D + 1 to D + 8 for the project as a whole. The unavailability of a large number of the tugs (125 instead of 200 planned) also meant that the transport was longer than expected and, consequently, the century's worst ever storm got hold of the Mulberry planned for Omaha and made it unusable. Arromanches, by this time, was almost complete and being better sheltered, it survived. It was later strengthened with the use of elements from Mulberry A Omaha to become the artificial port of the Liberation, used until November 1944 by the Royal Engineers. The total productivity of Admiral Tennant's A&B Mulberries did not however exceed 15 % of the total of the Allies' logistics in Normandy. This revelation led the Allied Chiefs of Staff to say that the landings and following military operations could have taken place just the same without the Mulberries, with no incidence on the final victory within the same time frame. Admiral Hall even declared that "the artificial ports demanded more efforts in time and in steel than they were of use !".

An aerial view of Mulberry B in Arromanches.

Arromanches : the Mulberry Harbour in August 1944. Note the concentration of equipment and access routes. ▶

ALLIED
TRANSPORT LOGISTICS

However, Mulberry A began operating on Omaha before Mulberry B, as early as the 16th June, to become on June 18th, the first European port ! 3.2 km long, 1.6 km deep, 15.5 million tons towed across the Channel by 97 tugs from the East of Southsea. The storm was to stop this strategic maritime plan in its tracks and on June 23rd, almost 800 naval units and numerous blocks of cement and metal lay along the 8 km of Omaha beach. 600 ships were, however, set afloat once again on the 8th July due to the efforts of the coastguards, the maritime engineers and the Navy, with 100 others following on July 25th.

Arromanches maintained an average 6,765 tons of supplies per day over the 5 months of operations. The beaches and Omaha in particular had the best productivity : 10 000 tons per day on Omaha from June 6th to September 30th, 5,000 tons per day on Utah, which was the beach on which most of Overlord's human resources landed with a total of 750,000 soldiers. Cherbourg was only to reach 10,000 tons per day from the end of August to November with a marked increase of 20,000 tons of freight landed on November 4th. By autumn, Cherbourg had become France's 2nd port after Marseille with some 2,826,740 tons arriving from the USA on 2,137 ships by VE Day ; these figures do

not, however, include the transport by trains or hospital ships of a large number of Anglo-American injured. In Cherbourg 148,753 injured were counted in transit over an 8-month period and 124,206 German POWs were exiled to the USA, the UK and Canada.

Omaha was closed on November 22nd 1944 and Utah on November 30th with the exception of a small number of transport activities carried out by DUKW's. Le Havre picked up after the two American beaches. In the Channel, still as dangerous as ever, mine hunting was to continue throughout the winter. Admiral Ramsay could have said, during the summer of 1944, that the daily tonnage in supplies handled by the American beaches, Arromanches and Cherbourg amounted to half of the total amount of the imports completed by the UK from the USA and the Commonwealth.

▲ Arromanches : a hospital ship and its ambulances alongside an LCT loaded with munitions.

An aerial view of the Mulberry Harbour in construction on Omaha Beach before the storm on the 19th July. ▶

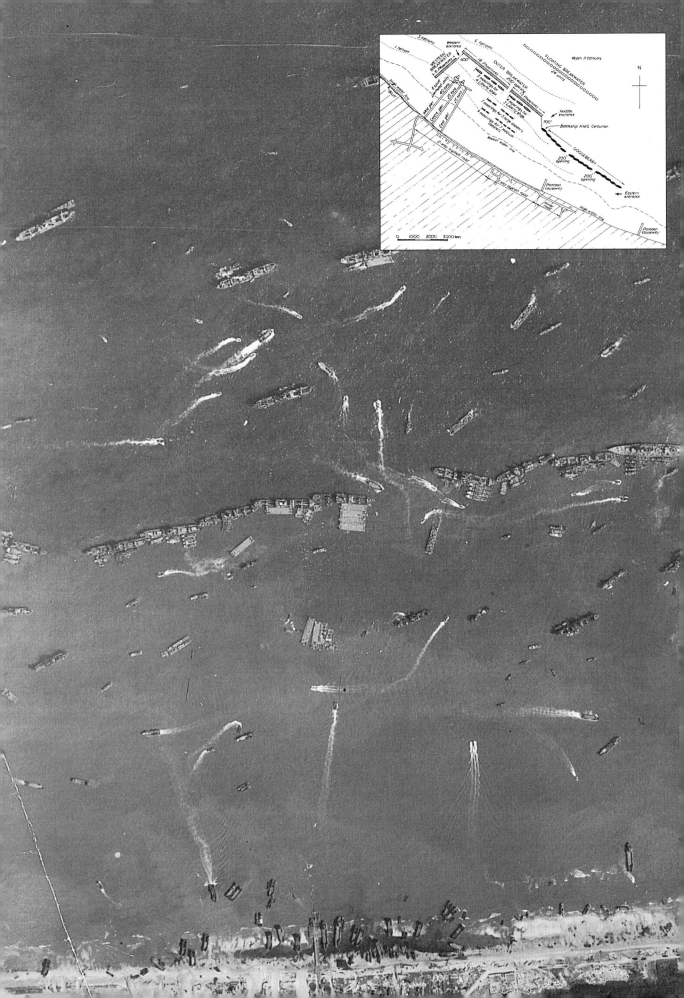

The LOGISTICS of THE MEDICAL CORPS and FOOD SUPPLIES

In the summer of 1944, the layer of sandy dust lay so thick inland from the beaches that green Normandy would no longer have been fit to be described as such, had it not been for the khaki mass of the Allied supply depots, protected from enemy air attacks by a load of green-coloured camouflage nets and browny-green artificial leaves. A large number of the crates hidden beneath this camouflage were the most precious Class I supplies : foodstuffs. The British depots were at Vaux-sur-Aure and in the sectors of the 4th and 11th Communication Lines of the 2nd British Army. The 10th Garrison's Headquarters were in Port-en-Bessin and the 12th Communications Line headquarters worked along with the 1st US Army Quarter Master Corps.

The water problem was resolved with, in July, 60 water points in working order operating from wells and rivers (Bayeux's drinking water was operational from June 11th onwards with a pumping station in Barbeville).

❶ THE MEDICAL CORPS

The main British sector medical zone, with 7 military hospitals, was located around Bayeux. 3 medical equipment depot bases were set up close to twelve general campaign hospitals inland from the beaches. Some, such as the one in Hermanville or Douvres, were supplied from a medical airfield located in Banville.

The chemical decontamination centres were used by the washing and mobile shower companies, always situated close to the water purifying centres. In Banville and Colleville, the "life shuttles" were operated by sanitary DC-3's, which brought the most essential supply into France – frozen blood supplies. The military blood bank was in Salisbury, a medical depot base, from where the precious refrigerated containers were transported by air. The provision of supplies by special, refrigerated means of transport to the advanced blood depots in Ryes and Littry was most difficult up until the beginning of August.

As soon as Cherbourg was re-opened, blood supplies were brought directly from the USA and transported as soon as was possible by railway to the front (Cherbourg, Lison on board the "Yankee Clipper").

The first 400 British female drivers from the Auxiliary Transport Corps landed in Arromanches on August 12th, following 4,200 Allied nurses from the 3 armed forces and preceding another female detachment of some 3,500 secretaries, medical auxiliaries, chefs, etc… From the 10th June to the 30th August 1944, all of the military hospitals belonging to the US Medical Department and the British and Canadian Royal Army Medical Corps treated a total 185,000 Allied patients and 40,000 German PW's.

▼ *Us medical trains in Carentan.*

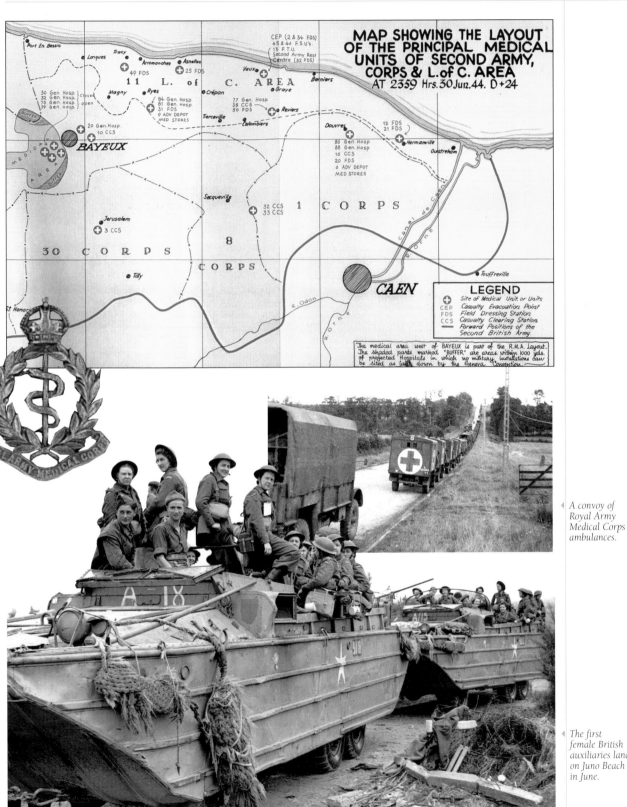

MAP SHOWING THE LAYOUT OF THE PRINCIPAL MEDICAL UNITS OF SECOND ARMY, CORPS & L. of C. AREA AT 2359 Hrs. 30 Jun. 44. D+24

LEGEND

✛	Site of Medical Unit. or Units
CEP	Casualty Evacuation Point
FDS	Field Dressing Station
CCS	Casualty Clearing Station
——	Forward Positions of the Second British Army.

The medical area west of BAYEUX is part of the R.M.A. Layout. The shaded parts marked "BUFFER" are areas within 1000 yds. of protected Hospitals in which no military installations can be sited as laid down by the Geneva Convention.

A convoy of Royal Army Medical Corps ambulances.

The first female British auxiliaries land on Juno Beach in June.

The LOGISTICS
of THE MEDICAL CORPS
and FOOD SUPPLIES

② FOOD SUPPLIES (CLASS I)

In the American sector, the Quarter Master Depots mainly provided the rations for the troops in operational zones.

These rations came in crates containing boxes of 48 smaller boxes split into 5 categories : C, K, D, B and A. They were delivered as a priority immediately after the first waves of the assault on D-Day. Four weeks later, 60 million rations pre-loaded in New York were landed and gathered together in depots inland from the beaches by the US 5th and 6th Engineers Brigades (Provisional Engineer Special Brigade Group) and those of the 11th Carriage Group of Omaha. Huge stocks were built up in the open air, along hedgerows, without totally managing to escape the sight of the more curious. Large sheets of tarred paper covered the tops of the piles which, at times, were 4 m high. All of the supplies were carefully camouflaged in June and July, then conspicuously left in the open at the end of August when the threat from the Luftwaffe had disappeared.

Fetching K-Rations in an American Class I Depot in Normandy.

Food was never lacking. Quite the contrary in fact, a very wide distribution of rations and bread was the gener during the 4 months of stocking supplies in Normandy.

Everyone, through fear of lacking food, pretended to have lost their stock, been unable to prevent a fire or a large shell from falling. This type of situation occurred to such an extent that the US Quarter Master and the Royal Army Service Corps were constantly required to transport hundr army corps tru the units engag combat and t 2 million men ved in August million who able to eat double serving liberators were also very ger with the civilian populatic soon as was possible, the included fresh vegetable dairy products, first of all de to the hospitals, then to th dren in the civilian refuge (Cully, Montebourg) and th the troops in the rest camps k the front line. The female s the US Food Departmen British Royal Army Catering and the Red Cross played a role in the organization of supplies, with the extra adv of boosting the troops' mora

In a field in the Manche County in Normandy,
an American infantry company receives its K-rations for 3 days.

US FOOD RATIONS

A rations : garrison rations based on perishable goods. They were only to reach Cherbourg directly from the USA in August. War rations from stocks gathered together in England were given priority.

WAR RATIONS

1) K Rations
These were composed of 3 units in rectangular cardboard boxes for :
a) breakfast unit with an egg, ham, a fruit bar and Nescafé ;
b) dinner unit with cheese and lemon flavoured powder ;
c) supper unit with meat, powdered soup, a bar of chocolate or D Ration. Each of the 3 units also contained packets of 5 cigarettes, chewing gum, sugar and a few biscuits.

2) C Rations
These were composed of 6 tins weighing 2.5 kg, containing 3 meals, to be reheated. They were not very popular as they were unpractical and contained : meat and vegetables in first 3 tins, sweets, cakes, Nescafé, lemon powder, chocolate and 50 cigarettes in the 3 others.

3) B Rations
These were the same as A rations without the perishable goods and in 10 in 1 packaging : cereals, milk, sugar, bacon, biscuits, jam and Nescafé for breakfast, a meal stew with beans and prunes for dinner. The GIs preferred these rations, which made up 70 % of the rations eaten by the American troops after July 15th.

4) D Rations or "Logan Bar"
This was the vitamined chocolate which was the favourite, not only of all the Allied troops, but also of the civilian population.

On July 25th, Class I supplies of food for the troops represented 48 % of the total supplies landed on the beaches (85 %) and the auxiliary ports (15 %). Transport of these supplies was ensured by the fleets of the army's main units, but, for 5 dramatic weeks after the pursuit during which the advance almost grinded to a halt because of a lack of trains and trucks, the Anglo-Canadian Transport Corps had to come to the rescue. This situation turned out to be to the great satisfaction of 1,500 drivers, who willingly exchanged their "Compo Rations" (for 14 men) for the American B rations and who forgot their Navy Cut cigarettes in favour of Chesterfields or Lucky Strikes.

Some of these supplies were delivered by parachute to isolated units, who could not be supplied by road : the British and US Airborne and also the "lost battalions" from Mortain or the Polish troops on Mont Ormel by the Falaise Gap (9th US Troop Carrier, RASC RAF Despatch Group).

The burying of refuse to preserve the ecology was a direct result of feeding 2 million soldiers during a campaign. Another more annoying result was the constant presence of swarms of bees, disturbed by the war and greatly attracted by foodstuffs, particularly American foods which contained more sweetener and these was nothing any A.A.Artillery could do about it. This was also the case for the clouds of mosquitos, attracted by this human tide and its refuse. The Allies hygiene units during the campaign had their work cut out and used tons of DDT and other formalin based products.

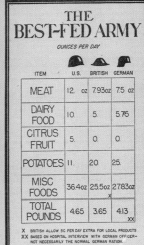

The 390th Engineers, 100 % black American, were responsible for American food supplies and landed on Utah on June 23rd. The black contingent in the American Army did not exceed 5 % in 1944. These soldiers mainly belonged to the "engineers" clearing and repairing roads. But they were represented even more in the COM-Z Corps, at the wheel of 6 x 6 GMCs and trailer trucks, where black Americans counted for 40 % of the 15,000 drivers of the communications network. Less involved in the fighting than the Canadians, countless "bronze stars" were nonetheless presented to the black contingent for exceptional valour during commanded service, even although the American Army did clearly make the segregationist distinctions which also applied in the States at the time.

▲ *Inland from Omaha, this American Class I supply depot is under construction.*

The SPECIAL CASE of BRITISH LOGISTICS

By the end of June, Cherbourg was liberated and the threat of enemy artillery fire was no longer to be feared by the Americans. It was not however quite the same story in the British sector :

1 - Le Havre only fell in September and the raids by motor torpedo-boats, human torpedo and explosive dinghy continued to create a climate of insecurity causing great damage to the Allied fleet (2nd August, 1 destroyer, 1LCG, 1 armed trawler, 3 LCTs either damaged or sunk) ;

2 - Enemy mobile artillery with 152 mm and 180 mm long range guns kept Sword Beach and the entrance to the port of Caen under sporadic, yet precise fire until the end of August ;

3 - German air bombing was carried out at night from the East and was not countered by the A.A.Artillery before reaching the fleet (flying bombs, BMC acoustic mines, remote controlled missiles, etc). Sword Beach remained in the front line until August 20th after which 1st British Corps cleared the Bay of Sallenelles to the Mont Canisy and Houlgate. It was for this reason that the landing of Anglo-Canadian logistics was essentially carried out in the sub-sector Mike, using, amongst other means, the small harbour in Courseulles. Gold Beach remained open on to the Asnelles-Meuvaine sector until Arromanches reached its cruising speed with some 6,000 tons of daily supplies. The fixing of the front compensated the delays in making up the stocks from the Gooseberries in Hermanville and Courseulles, where off-shore jetties enabled the unloading of small coasters and the shuttles carried out by the Royal Navy Service Corp's DUKWs. These beaches were exclusively used for Class I and V supplies (food and munitions), Port-en-Bessin having been used for fuel. 750,000 tons were thus landed by the Anglo-Canadians outwith the artificial harbour in Arromanches between 6th June and 20th August 1944 ; not forgetting the delivery of mail in all forms for the troops of the 2nd British Army from June 8th onwards ! Later the mail was brought to Normandy by sea, at a rate of 6,000 tons per day on Gold and Juno. On D + 10, 80,000 tons were in the depots, with a peak of 125,765 tons of varied British munitions on August 12th. The transport of munitions to artillery batteries was carried out by 2 ton-trucks, at times under enemy fire and almost 24 hours a day. The royal artillery seemed to devour 150 mm, 90mm and 105 mm American shells in June and July. One barrage fire during a British offensive used up 5,000 tons in 45 minutes !

The main offensives were not always successful, but were always costly in terms of the number of artillery projectiles used. As usual, the rear had to follow (operation Charnwood 3,000 tons, Jupiter 6,000 tons, Greenline 4,000 tons Goodwood 7,000 tons, Atlantic 2,000 tons, Spring 2,800 tons, Totalize 4,000 tons, Tractable 3,500 tons, Bluecoat 5,000 tons, etc…) over and above the offensives, there was forbidden fire on the limited German counter attacks, counter battery fire and concentrations on the meeting zones ("Stoncks" in heavy mortar, "Uncle" in the division, "Tare" in the Army Corps, "Victor" in the army as a whole. Whilst Patton advanced in leaps and bounds to the East (65 km per day), it was the Allied rear troops, who provided the immediate or secondary logistical means to do so. Was the well-disserved recognition of the work of the soldiers on logistics, who had to make do with Fieldmarshal Montgomery's congratulations at the end of the hostilities, not justly in accordance with the task they had accomplished ? The Royal Engineers, for their part, were responsible for mine clearance, building roads, bridges, the Port Winston in Arromanches, water and fuel logistics, all heavy tasks perfectly accomplished after 4 months' heavy labour in Normandy.

A British "Rhino" ferry transporting 20 trucks directly on to the beach, from a cargo ship anchored 2 miles out at sea.

Bulldozers, cranes belonging to the RAF Engineers

Parks and depots were required to stock German war equipment and munitions abandoned in huge quantities and often booby-trapped. On 10th September 1944, the number of mines lifted on land (and at sea by the Navy) around the Landing Beaches and invasion ports represented 13 % of the total number of mines used on all fronts during the length of the Second World War (Sept 1939 – Aug. 1945) ! 60 years on, these munitions are still dealt with by around 50 mine clearance specialists in France, who continue to clear 50 tons per year. Other French Naval teams also do mine clearing with an average of 10 tons per year at sea.

The Royal Engineers were also responsible for providing telephone cables for the Royal Army Signal Corps : apart from the underground cross-Channel cable laid as early as June 6th with 3 telephone and 6 telegraph circuits in the one cable. The Admiralty, the Signal Corps and the British Post Office maintained this telephone network, which stretched from London to Bayeux for a full year. Other cables were laid in July and August, achieving by September 30th 1944, a network of 160,000 km of telephone lines laid by the British.

▲ *A British signpost at the entrance to Bayeux on the N13 from Caen indicating the ring road avoiding the narrow streets in town and still know today as the by-pass.*

▲ *The Bayeux by-pass completed on June 27th by the Royal Engineers crossed the River Aure on Bailey Bridges.*

The SPECIAL CASE
of BRITISH
LOGISTICS

SUMMARY OF ANGLO-CANADIAN SERVICE ACTIVITIES (RE, RASC)

	SUPPLIES STATISTICS	LAND MEANS	TRANSPORT
Advanced maintenance sector (2 per army corps)	- 2 days' rations - 1 day's main stocks - 1.2 million litres of fuel - 3,500 tons munitions	- 2 supply depots - 2 service companies	Army Corps 1,000 tons/day
Army Depot Zone	- 10 to 20,000 tons of equipment in stock - 1 million litres of campaign jerrycans - 3 fuel filling stations	- 2 food supply depots - 5 fuel supply depots - 4 stationary depots - 4 bakery depots	Army 2,600 tons/day
Rear Maintenance Zone	- Ship unloading zone (DUKW) 2,000 tons/day - Beach maintenance zone	- Fuel installations (RASC) - 14 fuel supply depots - 6 mobile filling stations - 18 delivery stations - 8 reserve depots - 2 campaign bakeries - 8 mobile bakeries	Communication lines by the group of armies

To all of these various activities must be added the specific tasks of the Aviation-Engineers of the USAAF and RAF, with the construction of 41 airfields in 75 days and their maintenance : 10,000 tons of SMT, 2,000 tons of PSP take off plates, 800 km² of fields and meadows transformed into airfields for 2,000 planes supplying water, fuel, munitions and foodstuff for 90,000 airmen and their equipment.

By September 1st, 70 % of the 8th USAAF staff were located in France (51,000 men) with their own means of transport (IX AFSC Truck battalions) and they transported 35 million litres of avgas and 62,000 tons of supplies up until September 5th.

▲ *Near an RAF field, rolls of Hessian flooring due to be laid beneath the wiring on the surface of the runways.*

Female US Army Air Corps staff help unload the "red blood" of victory via the Red Ball Express.

On an American base in Normandy, this P47-D Thunderbolt fighter-bomber has three additional fuel tanks each containing 220 litres of fuel.
▼

◄ *An advanced RAF airfield in Normandy : here the B2 Bazenville-Crepon RAF/RCAF aifield. Note the convent in Villiers-le-Sec (used at the time as a home for veterans) in the bottom left hand corner.*

The SPECIAL CASE of BRITISH LOGISTICS

THE CONTROL OF WATER SUPPLIES

"Without water, life is impossible"
Given the important risk of the poisoning of water wells by the enemy during the landing operation, the Allies chose to bring sufficient quantities of drinking water for 150,000 men for 48 hours all the way from England. The ration was of 4 litres of water per man per day, with 8 litres in the medical units. The water treating equipment was landed from D + 1 by the engineers.
The individual treatment of water was done using chlorine "d'Halazone" tablets which were distributed to all the Allied formations landing in Normandy.

The Allied logistics planners organized the excellent water supply in Normandy with 10,000 men of the engineers who used river treatment equipment, electric pumping centres, thousands of tankers and other motor pumps. For every civilian installation repaired, 30 others were built from rivers, easily providing the precious liquid for the armed forces, their machines and hospitals, but also for the civilian population

recently liberated. This was the case in Cherbourg, Lison, Isigny, Carentan, Bayeux, each pump produced 100,000 litres per hour, which meant a total of 40 million litres per 24 hours in July on the whole of the bridgehead. The Royal Canadian Engineers operated the pumping and water stations on the River Orne in Fleury for the city of Caen, as soon as it was finally liberated on July 19th. The civilian population having taken refuge in the quarries in Fleury found that "the Canadian water was tasteless" after having spent weeks drinking water directly from the river. When there was no river at hand, the engineers drilled for water and around 100 pumping stations were thus created directly from ground water either for the use of the troops, a general hospital of 1,200 beds or an airfield, great users of water to spray the runways during the summer of 1944. The wells were most widely used by bucket waterwheels, motor pumps and tanker lorries ; in Hermanville, the well supplied 7 million litres in June and was later to figure in the British Army Order in justified recognition of the specific logistics of water supplying.

▲ *In Creully : treating the water of the River Seulles.*

▲
*Water supplies in the gardens
of St Gabriel castle.*

▶
*The well in Bretteville-l'Orgueilleuse is here well-used
by the 43rd DIV at the end of June 1944.*

EPILOGUE

The whirlwind of figures representing the huge logistics machine of the Western Allies must not allow us to forget that, despite their absolute material supremacy, it took an 11 month campaign to liberate Europe, from the Normandy Beaches to Berlin. However, even if the Allied Supreme Command did use the appropriate political and logistical means, the war on the Western front would probably have been shorter if :

- POLITICAL MEANS

The opportunity to capture both German armies encircled in the Falaise Gap had been fully seized. As it was, this only occurred to 25 % of the possibilities and enabled the retreat of considerable German forces. The same troops, rearmed made up the core of the Reich's defences and brutally counter-attacked the Americans and the French from the Belgian Ardennes to Alsace in December 1944. At the same time, Soviet troops could have gained the upper hand on the Eastern front and thus had more weight during the negotiations for their sharing of influence in Western Europe…

- LOGISTICAL MEANS

- *By doubling the vehicle fleet available for express transport. Paradoxically, the vehicles made available for the "Red Ball Express" were largely insufficient and did not enable the Allies to seize the opportunity to catch and disturb the enemy between the Rivers Seine and Meuse, at the beginning of September.*
- *By exclusively entrusting the air forces with the job of supplying the starving civilian population of Paris, rather than using road transport so crucially needed for the armies' war efforts*
- *By fairly distributing fuel to the Anglo-Canadians and to the Americans. By providing Montgomery with sufficient fuel to capture Le Havre, Calais and Boulogne and then opening other pipelines closer to the front, without stopping Patton's advance on the Rhine by shutting off his fuel supply.*

CONCLUSION

Whatever the reason, the 5 week period at the end of the summer of 1944, when all hope was possible, was not long enough to enable the necessary adjustments of the Allies' gigantic logistics machine. The technological and industrial assets, perfectly generated by the citizens of Western democracies and used to the best of their efficiency by other citizens in uniforms, were not sufficient to avoid another war, the Cold War between the former Eastern and Western Allies.

Appendices

THE FOUR PHASES
OF THE LIBERATION OF FRANCE

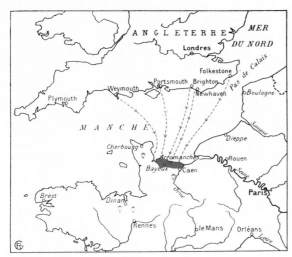

La situation au 10 juin.

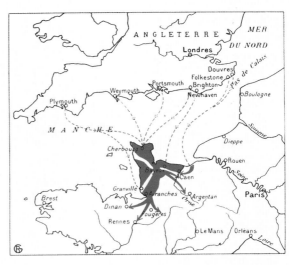

La situation au 31 juillet.

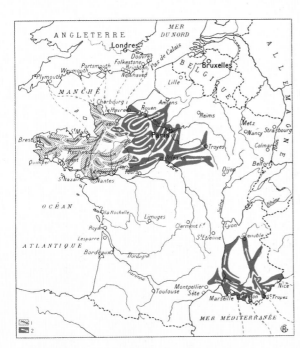

La situation au 31 août.

1. Opérations du 6 juin au 15 août. — 2. Opérations du 15 au 31 août.

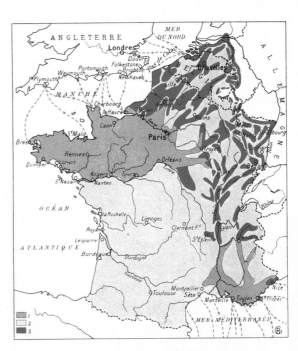

La situation au 31 décembre.

1. Territoires libérés au 31 août. — 2. Régions épargnées par la bataille.
3. Opérations du 1er septembre au 31 décembre.

QUATRE PHASES DE LA LIBÉRATION DE LA FRANCE

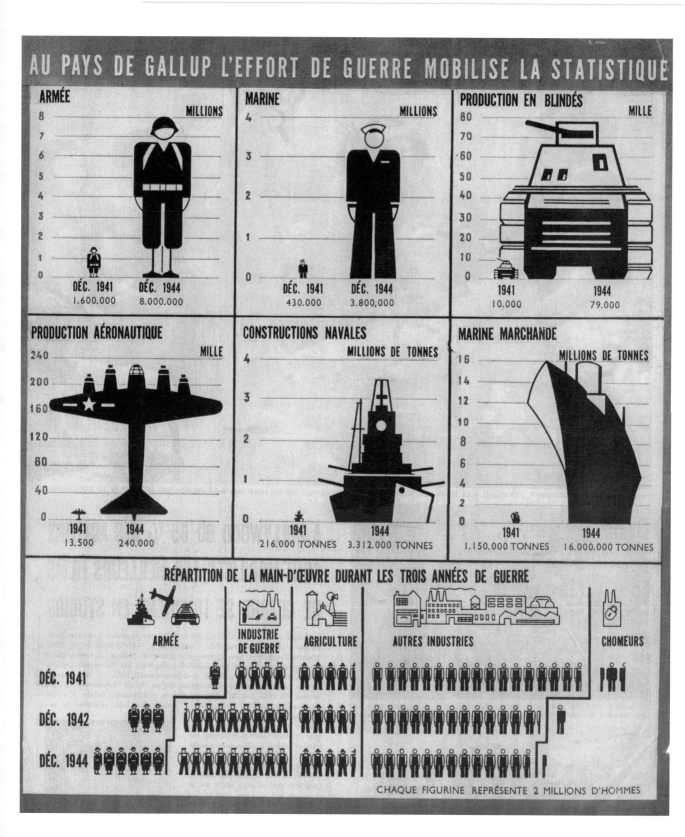

AU PAYS DE GALLUP L'EFFORT DE GUERRE MOBILISE LA STATISTIQUE

ARMÉE — MILLIONS

DÉC. 1941	DÉC. 1944
1.600.000	8.000.000

MARINE — MILLIONS

DÉC. 1941	DÉC. 1944
430.000	3.800.000

PRODUCTION EN BLINDÉS — MILLE

1941	1944
10.000	79.000

PRODUCTION AÉRONAUTIQUE — MILLE

1941	1944
13.500	240.000

CONSTRUCTIONS NAVALES — MILLIONS DE TONNES

1941	1944
216.000 TONNES	3.312.000 TONNES

MARINE MARCHANDE — MILLIONS DE TONNES

1941	1944
1.150.000 TONNES	16.000.000 TONNES

RÉPARTITION DE LA MAIN-D'ŒUVRE DURANT LES TROIS ANNÉES DE GUERRE

ARMÉE — INDUSTRIE DE GUERRE — AGRICULTURE — AUTRES INDUSTRIES — CHOMEURS

DÉC. 1941

DÉC. 1942

DÉC. 1944

CHAQUE FIGURINE REPRÉSENTE 2 MILLIONS D'HOMMES

G.I. Joe and his **12** tons of baggage

WHEN an American soldier goes overseas, between five and twelve *tons* of equipment must go with him. And . . .

Another ton must be sent to him *every* month, in food, clothing, and ammunition.

Who sees that he gets it?

The colossal task of supplying our millions of men is the responsibility of the *Army Service Forces*. Theirs is the job of designing, procuring, and transporting every item of Army equipment except airplanes and items peculiar to the Air Forces.

From the time a soldier is sworn in, until his discharge, the ASF takes care of him. It feeds him the world's best army food, and outfits him

with the finest clothing. It supplies him with the most modern weapons — guns, tanks, ammunition, trucks. And it carries on a vast research program to insure still better equipment.

The ASF delivers a soldier's mail, pays him, provides religious services for him, and gives him the best of medical care.

The ASF is the biggest business in history. It supplies some *half a million* different items, ranging from aspirin tablets to steamboats. Without batting an eye, the ASF fills rush orders from all over the world for stupendous quantities of materials.

Such orders as: 100 pneumatic drills, 40 pile drivers, 80 rock crushers, 100 tractors, 9000 prefabricated houses, 19 miles of 36-inch

metal pipe. And candy, louse powder, locomotives, cigarettes, books, and vaccines.

Because the outcome of battles depends so much on getting supplies *where* they are needed, *when* they are needed, the motto of the ASF is "Enough and On Time."

The amazingly efficient way in which the men of the ASF are living up to their motto has made today's American soldier the best-fed, best-clothed, best-equipped, and best-cared-for fighting man in history.

★ *Back the attack!—BUY MORE THAN BEFORE!* ★

INSIGNIA OF ARMY SERVICE FORCES

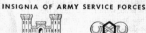

Quartermaster Corps   Ordnance Dept.   Corps of Engineers   Chemical Warfare Service   Signal Corps   Medical Corps

Judge Advocate General's Dept.   Chaplains (Christian and Jewish)   Military Police   Adjutant General's Dept.   Finance Dept.   Transportation Corps

SPERRY
CORPORATION
30 Rockefeller Plaza, New York 20

This message is published by Sperry to foster a wider appreciation of the Army Service Forces as the vital link between the production front and the fighting front. Sperry co-operates with the ASF through these divisions:

FORD INSTRUMENT CO., INC.
SPERRY GYROSCOPE CO., INC. • VICKERS, INC.
Waterbury Tool Division, VICKERS, INC.

101

Advertisement in the American magazine Life dating from July 1944 indicating that behind every GI, 12 tons of baggage was necessary.

Appendices

Emblem of the American Supply Corps for the campaign in North-West Europe.

COM-Z

Stage zone, this was the American logistics which pushed the army far from its bases of departure. It was also through these one way arteries and veins that messages, supplies, reinforcements for the front, the injured, prisoners, recuperation material to the rear were transported. This was the vital blood flow for the army, which if cut, would have caused the death of its main body. COM-Z dealt with everything which is not "combat".

ETOUSA

European Theatre Operation US Army. With over 12 million soldiers, the USA provided 2.3 million GIs for the European front. Out of a total population of 105 million inhabitants of working age, 60 million took part in the war effort in 1944

"QUARTER MASTER"

These services looked after the soldiers, fed them, clothed them, provided shelter, laundered them, provided them with fuel and all that was required for their military comfort. If a soldier died, this department was responsible for organizing his funeral and afterwards for looking after his grave. The US Quarter Master depots had over 70,000 articles in their inventory. 95% of all foodstaffs were brought from the USA. The Quarter Master Corps was also responsible for cleaning up the battlefield, recuperating anything which could be recuperated and repairing any damaged equipment.

THE ORDNANCE CORPS

This Corps was responsible for providing the armed forces with "anything which could be used to shoot, anything which could be rolled along the ground, anything which could be launched and anything which could be dropped from the air", including the maintenance, the reparation of this equipment and the repair of enemy equipment which could then be reused against the enemy. The weapons' service set up their workshops close to the front and moved their depots as they advanced. Many French workers gave precious assistance to the American Ordnance Corps (in Cherbourg, St Lô and Orleans).

THE ENGINEERS CORPS

This corps was responsible for construction and reparation. They repaired and built hundreds of kilometres of roads and railways, repaired 172 bridges, built 320 others, set 14 ports back in working order and laid pipelines from the beaches to the front. They destroyed thousands of mines, demolished buildings which were likely to collapse, built 80 airfields, often with the help of local manpower.

THE TRANSPORTATION CORPS

This department was responsible for the landing of the troops and their equipment. It was the Transportation Corps' job to transport the men and equipment, using the roads cleared by the Engineers Corps, as far as the front within the set timescale. They were also in charge of transporting the injured to the evacuation centres. It was this Corps which installed the famous "Red Ball Express" circuit over a period of 80 days with 6,000 trucks providing some 500,000 tons of equipment and freight from the Normandy beaches to the front line and back again.

PROVOST MARSHALL

The Provost Marshalls controlled the traffic, often exposed to enemy fire directing vehicles and ensuring a free run for priority vehicles. They were also responsible for prisoners of war and temporarily, for the control of recently liberated civilians. In the US Army, they ensured the discipline amongst the troops.

SIGNAL CORPS

Radio-telephone transmissions and telegraph transmissions were the main role of the Signal Corps. They were also responsible for the photographic and film archives providing us with the images of the war. Their motorcyclists carried written orders and they repaired some 700,000 French telephone lines which had been destroyed. They equipped 107 headquarters with teleprinters, which could send, using perforated tapes, some 68 words per minute on average a distance of 300 km without any relay being required.

US MEDICAL DEPARTMENT

The Medical Department was present at the front providing first aid to the injured before transferring them to medical centres. Campaign hospitals then took over, treating those who could be treated and sending the more seriously injured to evacuation centres, which in turn ensured the patients return, by air or sea, to the U.K. or to the U.S.A. Any emergency operations were always carried out on the battlefields in general campaign hospitals.

SPECIAL SERVICES

These services were responsible for the moral of the troops. This department published forces' newspaper and provided bibles and books for the soldiers. They provided communication with the rest of the country through radio and cinema productions. They brought in the most popular American stars to perform and entertain the troops (Marlene Dietrich, Greta Garbo, Bob Hope, Frank Sinatra, Fred Astair and Ginger Rogers). An American soldier needed to know what he's fighting for, he considered himself to be a citizen in uniform, who needed to be kept informed, educated, to take part in his religion, to play sport and watch films and attend theatre productions which he liked. Ensuring all of the above was the job of the Special Services, who did so with the most eclectic staff, from the stars of stage and screen to the padre, all united with the same aim of keeping the moral and physical health of the American and French troops at their best ; the French troops attached to the American forces were General Leclerc's 2nd DB and a large part of De Lattre de Tassigny's 1st French Army which landed in Provence on the 15th August 1944.

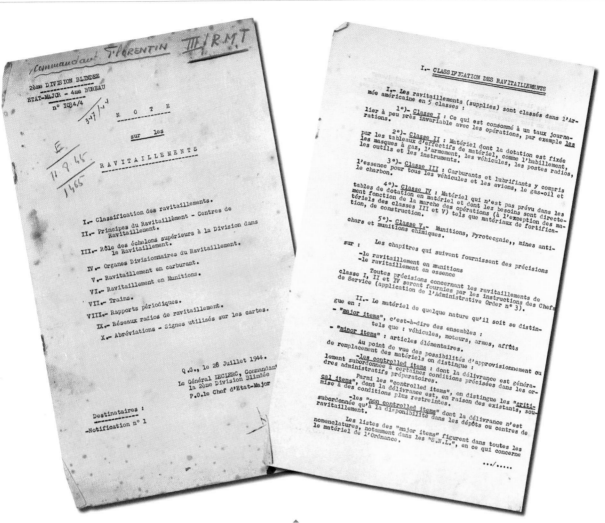

*American supplies classifications for the 2nd French Armoured Division,
which landed on August 1st 1944 on Utah Beach, under the command of General Patton's 3rd US Army.
These documents were for the 3rd infantry battalion of the Teliad marching regiment,
signed by the commanding officer of the 2nd DB, General Leclerc.*

◀ *Emblem of the French 2nd DB.*

◀ *Signs of the European highway code to be transferred to the windscreens of the Allied COM-Z vehicles.*

Appendices

American technical manuals in French printed in the USA for the rearming of the French army, $as early as November 1942, on the occasion of the first return to the Mediterranean by US. Since 1940, the Landings in North Africa, codenamed operation "Torch" under the command of Generals Eisenhower, Patton and Bradley

FM 17–50 (French)

MINISTERE DE LA GUERRE

MANUEL DE CAMPAGNE DES FORCES BLINDEES

RAVITAILLEMENT ET TRANSPORT

3 Juin, 1943

FM 17–57 (French)

MINISTERE DE LA GUERRE

MANUEL DE CAMPAGNE DES FORCES BLINDEES

BATAILLON DE RAVITAILLEMENT D'UNE DIVISION BLINDEE

le 9 avril 1943

ANNEXE II

S-4 PERIODIC REPORT

From _____ (Date/Hour)
To _____ (Date/Hour)
Reporting Unit _____
Location Unit _____
Date and Hour _____

NUMBER _____.

Maps - Reference _____

1.— LOCATION OF ADMINISTRATIVE TROOPS AND INSTALLATIONS (Use overlay or map showing disposition, or list organizations, locations and map coordinates): (Le Btn Medical, le GER 35 et la Grd.d'Exploitation doivent mentionner dans ce paragraphe l'emplacement de leurs Unités)

2.— STATUS OF SUPPLY.

a. Class I (Ce paragraphe n'est a remplir que par l'Intendant)
Ration Strength _____

List in applicable column below the amount (number) of various types of rations on hand including reserves and the number of rations, broken down by the various types, that were received during the period covered by this report.

TYPE	On Hand in Unit Including Reserve	On Hand in Dumps	On Hand in Depots	On hand Distributing Point	Rations Received during Period covered by this Report
"A"					
"B"					
"C"					
"D"					
"K"					
10-in-1					
5-in-1					

b. Class II (Ce par.est a remplir par tous les Chefs de Corps ou Cdts d'unite formant Corps) List in applicable columns below critical shortages by Supply Service. Use extra pages if necessary.

Supply Service	Item	Auth.	On hand in Unit Including Reserves	On Hand in Dumps	On Hand in Depots	On Hand Distributing Points
				A ne pas remplir par les Corps		

Weapons, all types, replaced during period covered by this report _____

.../.....

---

c. Class III (ce paragraphe est a remplir par la Base pour la Section de transport d'essence, par tous les Chefs de Corps et Commandants d'Unités formant Corps)

FUEL (Gallons)	On Hand	Days of Supply @ 50 Miles per Day	Consumed during period covered by Report	Received during Period covered by Report
Gasoline V-100				
Gasoline V-80		Cette colonne n'est pas a remplir par les Corps		
Diesel Fuel				
Kerosene				
OIL (Gallons)				
SAE				
SAE				
SAE				
SAE				
SAE				
GREASE (Lbs)				
Type				
Type				
Type				
Type				

d. Class IV (a remplir par tous les chefs de Corps et Cdts d'Unite formant Corps)

List in applicable column below Critical Shortage and Major Stockages on hand. Use extra pages if necessary

Supply Service	Item	Auth.	On Hand in Unit Including Reserves	On Hand in Dumps	On Hand in Depots	On hand Distributing Points
					A ne pas remplir par les Corps	

e. Class V (a remplir par Corps et Unites formant Corps) par la Base en ce qui concerne la 5e colonne.

List in applicable columns below Critical Shortages and Ammunition Expended during period covered by this Report. Use extra pages if necessary.

Supply Service	Item	Auth.	On Hand in Unit Including reserves	On Hand in Dumps	On hand in Depots	On hand Distributing Points	Expended During Period
				A remplir par Base reserve sur roues ou Train	A ne pas remplir		

.../.....

Us accounting form for class I food supplies, class II equipment in French and in English. Here for General Leclerc's 2nd DB : class III poil and fuel, class V munition and other class IV material for the engineers.

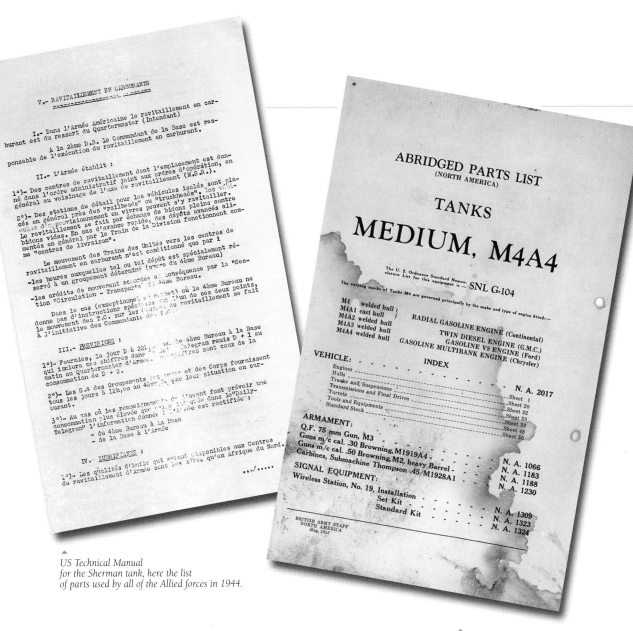

US Technical Manual
for the Sherman tank, here the list
of parts used by all of the Allied forces in 1944.

Document belonging to the French
2nd DB, set on the American model,
concerning fuel supplies which could
reach some 500,000 litres per day
during the advance.

Individual American rations' cards for
the supply of Class II canteen accessories
(razor blades, matches, chewing-gum, etc.),
distributed to troops in England
before they left for France.

Appendices

Technical Manual
of the Royal British Armoured Corps
for the maintenance of Churchill tanks.

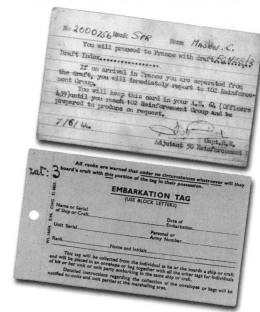

▲ List of Class I British rations for D-Day, 6th June 1944.

Caption in Newsweek on June 7th 1944 :
"you can't say we didn't tell you we'd be back".

Exceptional distribution of special food rations
for Anglo-Canadian D-Day troops.

HEADQUARTERS SECOND ARMY

ISSUE OF SPECIAL ITEMS

1. Certain items of special rations and equipment are being issued by the Camp Commandant to all personnel prior to embarkation.

2. There is a reason for the issue of each separate item. These reasons are given below so that all offrs and other ranks are aware of the importance of the issue.

3. The items are NOT replaceable, and care must be taken against loss.

4. Any personnel found to have consumed any item of the issue before the appointed time will be liable to severe disciplinary action.

24 Hour Ration Packs.

All personnel are issued with two 24 hr ration packs with the exception of those landing on D Day who are issued with one 24 hr ration Pack (Type 'A') and one 24 hr ration pack (not type 'A').

These, together with a Tommy Cooker and a water sterilizing outfit are for the first 48 hrs of landing. They must not be consumed before landing as no other rations will be available.

EMERGENCY RATION

Not to be consumed under any circumstances unless no other form of subsistence is available and then only upon orders of an offr.

PRESERVED MEAT

One tin is issued to all personnel landing up to and including D + 2, to supplement the two 24 hr ration packs.

CHEWING GUM

Personnel landing on D Day, get a packet of Chewing Gum each to alleviate sea sickness during the voyage.

BISCUITS AND CHOCOLATE

All offrs and ORs are issued with a packet of biscuits and two bars of chocolate. These are for consumption during the period between leaving for embarkation and actually arriving on board.

MATCHES

No matches are available for issue. All ranks are advised to obtain at least one box of matches under private arrangements and to carry them wrapped in some waterproof material.

BAGS, VOMIT

Issued on the scale of three per officer and other rank.

Chevrolet-built Pratt & Whitney engines power America's mightiest warplanes, including the C-82 Flying Boxcar, shown above.

CHEVROLET

America's Automotive Leader Gears All Its Resources to

THE BIGGEST TRANSPORT JOB OF ALL TIME"

on land ··· in the air ··· all around the world

...Y MORE WAR BONDS
...LP SPEED THE VICTORY

Chevrolet has produced more than 475,000 military trucks in three different types, serving our fighting men everywhere.

CHEVROLET DIVISION OF GENERAL MOTORS

U.S. ROYAL
De Luxe

KEEP AMERICA'S CARS ROLLING

Rolling over the battlefields of the world and the highways of home—every car is a war car now. Your car is a war car and its tires are tools of war just as truly as if they were rolling on tanks or guns or bombers.

Today, true to tradition, U. S. Tires are serving over and beyond the line of duty to keep America's cars rolling. Like your local, independent U. S. Tire Dealer—they are making every tire mile count—toward victory.

IN EVERY SERVICE, U. S. TIRES EXCEL!

U.S. TIRES

To make every tire mile count—stop at this sign of skilled service.

It identifies a local, independent business built on experience, knowledge and products of quality.

 UNITED STATES RUBBER COMPANY

1230 SIXTH AVENUE, ROCKEFELLER CENTER, NEW YORK 20, N. Y. • In Canada: DOMINION RUBBER CO., Ltd.

Serving Through Science *Listen to "Science Looks Forward"—new series of talks by the great scientists of America—on the Philharmonic-Symphony Program. CBS network, Sunday afternoon, 3:00 to 4:30 E.W.T.*

Bibliography

General DD Eisenhower	▸ Crusade in Europe
	▸ The operations of the Allied Expeditionary Forces in Europe
General Charles De Gaulle	▸ Mémoires de guerre – Vol 1
General Pakenwam-Walsh	▸ History of the Corps of Royal Engineers – Vol IX
Colonel R. Leigh	▸ American Enterprise in Europe
R. Ruppenthal	▸ Logistical Support of the Armies – Vol I
M. Blumenson	▸ Patton's papers
Keith and Rosenthal	▸ The Corps of Engineers, troops & equipment
Bell	▸ The story of the RASC 1939-45
H.M. Stationnery Office	▸ Invasion Europe
Benamou & Robinard	▸ La Bataille Aérienne de Normandie
HMSO	▸ Administrative History of 21st Army-Group
	▸ 8 June 44 – 8 May 45
Pogue	▸ The Supreme Command
United States Information Service	▸ COM-Z

Iconography

US Army photos	▸ Pages : 2, 8, 10, 14, 22, 22 bottom, 24, 25, 26, 27 bottom, 29 bottom, 33 top, 35 bottom, 38 top, 43, 44, 56, 58, 60, 63 top / JPB
National Archives USA	▸ Pages : 6, 7 top, 9 top, 23 top, 32 top & bottom, 39, 40, 41, 42 top, 48 bottom, 49, 50 top and middle, 51, 52 top and middle, 53, 65 top and middle / JPB
Imperial war museum (London)	▸ Pages : 17 top and bottom, 30, 60, 61 bottom, 62, 64, 66, 67 / JPB
Canadian Public Archives	▸ Pages : 20, 21, 48 top, 57, 59 bottom / JPB
Archives Musée du Débarquement Arromanches	▸ Pages : 4, 5, 11, 12/13 bottom, 34, 52, 54, 56
J.P. Bénamou Archives	▸ Pages : cover, 1, 6, 7 bottom, 9 bottom and middle, 12/13 top, 16, 18, 19, 23 bottom, 24 bottom, 27 top and middle, 28, 29 top, 30 bottom, 31, 33 bottom, 34, 35 top, 36, 37, 42 bottom, 45, 46, 47, 50 bottom, 52 bottom, 55, 59 middle, 61, 63, 65 bottom, 67, 68, 70, 71, inside cover. Emblems and documents / JBP Archives.

OREP

E D I T I O N S

15, rue de Largerie - 14480 Cully
Tél. (33) 02 31 08 31 08
Fax : (33) 02 31 08 31 09
info@orep-pub.com

Graphic Design : OREP
ISBN : 2-912925-36-3
Copyright OREP 2003
All Rights Reserved

Legal deposit : 2nd term 2003

Printed in France